A TOAST TO THE FUR TRADE

"TO THE FUR TRADE IN ALL ITS BRANCHES" was one of five toasts regularly proposed at the Beaver Club dinners in Montreal. Other toasts were:

"To the Mother of All Saints"
"To the King"
"To Voyageurs, Wives and Children"
"To Absent Members"

The club was formed in 1785 by nineteen fur traders, each of whom had spent at least one winter in the *pays d'en haut* (upper country). There were eight French-speaking members, six Scots, two Americans, and three Englishmen. Among the charter members were Charles Chaboilliz (first voyage to the interior, 1751); Maurice Blondeau, 1752; Alexander Henry, 1761; James McGill, 1766; Joseph Frobisher, 1768; and Peter Pond, 1770.

One of the main objects of the club was "to bring together, at stated periods during the winter season, a set of men highly respectable in society who had spent their best days in a savage country, and had encountered the difficulties and dangers incident to a pursuit peculiar to the fur trade of Canada."

The regular meetings began the first week in December and were held once a fortnight until the second week in April. At one memorable dinner in 1797, attended by Alexander Mackenzie and William McGillivray of the North West Company, the members were still singing, dancing, drinking, and boasting at 4:00 a.m. One hundred and twenty bottles of wine were either drunk or spilled that evening. There were about twenty present.

[Clifford P. Wilson, "The Beaver Club," *The Beaver*, March, 1936.]

A Toast to the Fur Trade

A Picture Essay on Its Material Culture

by Robert C. Wheeler

Illustrations by David Christofferson

Edited by Ardis Hillman Wheeler

Designed by Robert N. Taylor

Wheeler Productions

WHEELER PRODUCTIONS, publisher

Library of Congress No. 84-091414
ISBN Hard cover 0-9614362-0-4   Paperback 0-9614362-1-2

To Marie Gérin-Lajoie
for her long friendship
and her many contributions
to this volume

Acknowledgments

This book would not have been possible without the help and kindness of many people and institutions. It is extremely fortunate that through the contacts and friendships developed over the years, especially in connection with my work on the Quetico-Superior Underwater Search for Fur Trade Artifacts, the trips into remote parts of Canada (many of which were to fur-trade sites, like Fort Albany, Rupert House, Fort Chipewyan and others) and my involvement in several North American Fur Trade Conferences, I have come to know many fine people who share a common interest in the fur trade. I am deeply grateful to the following who have given me invaluable assistance: Douglas Birk, archaeologist, for checking the illustrations and manuscript for accuracy and offering valuable suggestions; Charles Diesen, conservator of the Minnesota Historical Society, for making available for photographing the fur-trade artifacts in the Society's collection; Jean Morrison, historian for Old Fort William, for furnishing information and suggestions; Patricia Harpole, chief of the Minnesota Historical Society's reference library, and her accommodating assistants, Wiley Pope and Alissa Wiener, for providing helpful source material; Alan R. Woolworth, archaeologist and research fellow of the Minnesota Historical Society, for information on Grand Portage; Jocylin McKillop and Helen Burgess, Hudson's Bay Company, for assisting on many aspects of the Company's history; Shirlee A. Smith, keeper of the Hudson's Bay Company records, for continued help and encouragement; Marcia Anderson, Minnesota Historical Society's museum curator, for making available items from the Society's collection; Warren Baker, Montreal collector, for providing rare material from his collection; Karlis Karklins, for a listing of major fur-trade sites in Canada; Charles Hanson, Jr., of Chadron, Nebraska, for information on trade guns. I am especially indebted to the Hudson's Bay Company for permission to quote from its records, and, of course, to Marie Gérin-Lajoie.

Others who have assisted with fur-trade artifacts and/or information are: Walter A. Kenyon, former curator of archaeology, Royal Ontario Museum; Hugh Macmillan, Nor'Westers and Loyalist Museum; Jeffrey P.

Brain, archaeologist, Peabody Museum, Harvard; Eric Morse, author of *Fur Trade Canoe Routes of Canada/Then and Now*; Edgar S. Oerichbauer, Wisconsin archaeologist; John Rivard, founder and former president, French-Canadian Society of Minnesota, and direct descendant of a French voyageur; Public Archives of Canada; Old Fort William staff, Thunder Bay, Ontario; McCord Museum of McGill University, Montreal; Glenbow Museum, Calgary, Alberta; National Museum of Man, Ottawa, Canada. A special thanks to Edna V. Carlson, a former secretary, who graciously volunteered to type the manuscript.

I am especially indebted to my wife, Ardis Hillman Wheeler, who not only served as editor of this volume but offered the encouragement needed to complete it; and our daughter, Kristi Wheeler Duckwall, a writer who was an additional sounding board.

Foreword

The primary purpose of this book is to bring to scholars, students of the fur trade, and others who find its history fascinating, the information I have collected over the years on the subject. With the material culture of the fur trade my main interest, I wish to demonstrate the importance of bringing together the object or artifact with the other sources of history, in order better to understand the past. I want also to underscore the significant role of the historical archaeologist and the museum specialist who must analyze the objects for the historian and help to interpret them for the museum or historic-site visitor.

For too long the professional historian neglected the three-dimensional object as of little or no use in the understanding of man's past. Happily that situation is changing. Marius Barbeau, a Canadian folklorist, more than a half-century ago, made a major plea for detailed study of European folk cultures in North America. In the United States, Carl P. Russell, an historian for the National Park Service, and like Barbeau, a pioneer in advocating the importance of studying material culture, said in a letter to me in 1963: "So far as I know, during 20 years, no one has moved toward an effective, organized program recognizing historic objects as sources of history . . . Really, there is a small fraternity within the world of archaeology-history which at present is unidentified among museums, universities, and other learned groups. It is a fraternity which should grow and which should be recognized *now*."

Another pioneer advocate of objects as "documents" was Carl Russell Fish, who, in a paper presented in Madison, Wisconsin, in 1910, said: "The first duty of the archaeologist is to discover such material and to verify it; the next is to secure its preservation. . . . Then comes the task of studying it; classifying it and arranging it, and making it ready for use. At this point the function of the archaeologist ceases and the duty of the historian begins; i.e., to interpret it . . . "

Man's creations (material culture) are key to an understanding of his needs, aspirations, interests, skills, thinking processes, and accomplishments. Very often the written record alone fails to report certain aspects of history found only in artifacts—tools, art, architecture, and other creations of man. Alexander J. Wall, in an address entitled "The Voice of the Artifact," given at the thirty-second annual meeting of the American Association for State and Local History in 1972, said: "The role of the historical artifact is more secure than ever before and is recognized as a necessary addition to the written record. It has become obvious that reliance on the written record alone can give just as incomplete a story as reliance solely upon an isolated artifact. It is the author's view that three-dimension artifacts include objects of any size, for example, historic buildings, steam locomotives and the remains of fur trading posts."

Ivor Noël Hume, director of the department of archaeology at Colonial Williamsburg, in his book *A Guide to Artifacts of Colonial America*, page 3, writes: " . . . as the Minnesota Historical Society has demonstrated, a collection of copper kettles or a cloth bag of files recovered by divers can bring portage history to life in a way that no document can ever achieve."

A secondary purpose of the book is to stress the importance of geography in the understanding of history. Elliott Coues, editor of the *Manuscript Journals of Alexander Henry and David Thompson, 1799–1814*, Vol. I, page xvii, writes: "The trouble seems to be that the best geographers have seldom been historians, while historians so good that they would blush to be caught afoul of a date wrong by a day are often found miles out of the way in the location of their events." D. G. G. Kerr, Professor of History at the University of Western Ontario, in his *A Historical Atlas of Canada*, page viii, says: "Canadian history includes much that can be fully understood only in relation to its geographical environment. This is true in particular of such topics as explorations, the spread of settlement, the development of trade and transportation routes . . . " Certainly then, this would be true of the fur trade and the vast areas it covered.

In my long career in historical society work, there were experiences with historical objects, historical archaeology, and geography which had a profound influence on my beliefs. Oddly enough, the first experience was years ago on a project involving the construction of teaching aids for the blind, many of which were of an historical nature—scaled models of Independence Hall, the White House, Thomas Jefferson's Monticello, and others. The second experience was working with the originals of this nation's early newspapers which reported important historical events as well as the mundane day-to-day activities in the settlements. School children were fascinated to see these documents first hand. In a real sense, they were objects as well as documents. Further in my career was another experience which strengthened my belief in the power of the artifact—collecting historical objects for the Ohio Historical Society: pioneer farm equipment, tools of early craftsmen, even a mid-nineteenth century gunshop complete with a few of the guns the gunsmith had made.

In Minnesota, as co-director of the Quetico-Superior Underwater Research Project, a program involving divers searching for early fur-trade materials, the objects lying on the bottom for two hundred years spoke forcefully to me. Finally, in the development of the Minnesota Historical Society's Forest History Center, where all the resources of history were brought into play—objects, photographs, the written records, as well as oral history—it became clear how necessary all are if we are fully to understand and interpret our past.

During twenty-one years with the Minnesota Historical Society, I had the opportunity to lead members on tours to various parts of the world to visit historic places. Some of these were to fur-trade sites in both Canada and the United States—Grand Portage, Fort William, Fort Albany, Rupert House, Moose Factory, Cumberland House, Norway House, Fort Chipewyan, York Factory, and others. Standing on the spot, examining the terrain, and sensing the remoteness, one comes to have a greater appreciation and understanding of the events which took place there. This appreciation and understanding I hope to impart.

NOTE: Brief references to sources quoted throughout the text will be enclosed in brackets. For more complete information consult the bibliography.

Contents

A TOAST TO THE FUR TRADE

Historical Introduction

It has been said that the fur trade unrolled the map of Canada. The same can be said of the map of much of the United States. An extraordinary set of circumstances contributed to the development of the trade:

1. The Indian wanted the white man's iron and cloth, and the European wanted the Indian's furs—a fair exchange.

2. The geography of the country lent itself to travel by water literally from coast to coast by a chain of navigable rivers and lakes which, for the most part, passed through the prime fur areas.

3. Along this extraordinary system of waterways grew the paper birch and the aspen trees. The birch provided the material for the bark canoe, and the aspen provided the primary food of the beaver—a fortunate combination.

4. Added to these factors was a climate which produced the finest furs.

Exactly when the fur trade began can only be surmised, but when it commenced in earnest is a matter of historical record. In the late fifteenth and early sixteenth centuries, navigators from the countries of Europe were probing the coastline of North America, seeking a short, high-latitude route to the Indies. The kings of Europe, intent on finding a route to China and seeking precious metals to add to coffers depleted by prolonged war, continued to send ships to the New World. To John Cabot goes the honor of being the first "discoverer" of the mainland, 1497, after the Vikings some five centuries earlier. Spain, following the voyages of Columbus, had concentrated on the areas to the south: Panama and Puerto Rico in 1508, Jamaica in 1509, Cuba in 1511, the islands of Venezuela in 1515, Mexico in 1519—this was the sequence of conquest. To the Spaniards went the riches of gold and silver. France and England, envious, had hoped that their explorations to the north would produce similar results. Their fortunes, however, would lie with "soft gold"—furs.

At some unknown time, shortly before or after the voyages of Columbus and Cabot, fishermen from the Catholic countries of Europe sailed into the fog-shrouded waters off Newfoundland, one of the finest and most productive fishing grounds in the world. With no refrigeration, their excellent catches of cod had to be preserved by salting or drying, and it was the drying which took the fishermen to shore. There they came in contact with the Indians. According to Samuel Eliot Morison in his *The European Discovery of America: The Northern Voyages, A.D. 500–1600*, page 265, "By 1523 it is possible to name several fishing vessels from La Rochelle [France] that were fishing on the Newfoundland Grand Banks." Jacques Cartier, discovering, as he thought, the Gulf of St. Lawrence in June, 1534, found a fishing vessel from La Rochelle there ahead of him. Cartier in July reports that natives approached his ship "brandishing peltry on sticks—a sure sign that European fishermen had been there before. . . . We made them signs that we wished them no harm," wrote Cartier, "and sent two men ashore to deal with them, bringing knives and other cutlery, and a red cap to give to their chief." The Indians responded with peltry and strips of broiled seal meat. According to Cartier, the natives, in return for gifts of hatchets, knives, paternoster beads, and other merchandise, gave furs they wore, and returned completely naked. Thus, with these and other brief encounters with explorers and fishermen, the fur trade in North America began. [Morison, pages 369–370.]

Before the end of the sixteenth century, the trading of merchandise for fur became more intensive and business-like, with all Indian-European exchanges taking place along the banks of the St. Lawrence River. Indians from the interior, coming great distances down the tributary rivers in their bark canoes, brought furs and returned to their villages with hatchets, knives, kettles, and beads to trade with even more remote tribes. "Archaeological evidence suggests that the Hurons were already part of a trade in European goods in the second half of the sixteenth century, and some connections probably existed with the St. Lawrence Iroquoians." [E. Palmer Patterson II, *The Canadian Indian: A History since 1500*, page 67.]

Marcel Trudel in his *The Beginnings of New France, 1524–1663*, page 79, states: "French goods that the Algonquins acquired by barter in the St. Lawrence were finding their way up the Ottawa River into the land of the Hurons. The sixteenth century had barely come to a close, and already European articles, mostly of metal, were reaching the natives of the interior some fifteen hundred miles from the Atlantic coast." These articles were traded by Indian middlemen. It is no wonder that these native entrepreneurs made every effort to prevent the Europeans from moving inland to trade. Frequently, remote Indian tribes would give all their beaver robes to the middlemen for old knives, blunted awls, wretched nets and kettles used until they were past service.

It was Samuel Champlain, one of the most famous men in French Canadian history, who began the push westward from the St. Lawrence up the Ottawa River. It was he who advocated the use of the cedar and birch-bark Indian canoes with which, he said, "one may travel freely and quickly throughout the country." Appropriately called the "father of the fur trade," Champlain in 1608 had sent a young man of twenty-three, Etienne Brulé to live with the Hurons and Algonquin Indians for the purpose of learning their language and routes to the interior country. "In 1603, Indians who could be understood gave the French the first description of the *pays d'en haut* [upper country] that clearly corresponded with reality." [Marcel Trudel, *The Beginnings of New France, 1524–1663*, page 78.] In 1615 Champlain and his interpreter, Brulé, traveled up the Ottawa and Mattawa rivers and thence westward down the French River to Georgian Bay. Brulé himself by 1621 had seen the eastern end of Lake Superior.

The full potential of the fur trade was perhaps not realized until the master *coureurs de bois* (woods runners)—Pierre Esprit Radisson and Medart Chouart, Sieur des Groseilliers—returned to Montreal in 1656 with great quantities of furs and reported to French officials the tremendous potential of engaging in the inland trade from Hudson Bay—all of which they had learned from Indians north of Lake Superior. The French officials, however, turned a deaf ear to Radisson and his companion, and so the two took their proposal to the English. The Hudson's Bay Company of Adventurers, chartered in 1670, was the result.

For the first hundred years, the Hudson's Bay Company built their posts on the periphery of the Bay—Fort Charles (later to become Rupert House), Moose Fort, Albany Fort, York Fort—all situated at or near the mouths of rivers emptying into Hudson Bay. Supplied by ships annually from England, the traders simply waited for the natives from the interior to bring their furs down the rivers in their canoes to the Bay. All went well for the English until the French traders, moving westward out of Montreal, began intercepting the Indians upriver, cutting off the flow of furs. To appreciate fully the effect this had upon the Hudson's Bay Company, one must understand the geography of the country west of the St. Lawrence, and particularly that around Hudson Bay. Imagine Hudson Bay as the hub of a wheel with the spokes the large rivers flowing into the Bay from all directions. With the gradual movement of the French traders westward along the Ottawa River, through the Great Lakes, and into the Northwest, most rivers leading to the Bay were crossed, with the French intercepting the trade—first, the Abitibi and the Moose, the Nipigon, the Albany, and finally the Saskatchewan (the last having a devastating effect on the trade at York Fort). The traders from Montreal were skimming off the best furs like marten, beaver and otter, leaving the coarser, less desirable pelts for the English.

In 1688 Jacques de Noyon, a French *coureur de bois*, reached Rainy Lake by way of the Kaministiquia River from Lake Superior, a route which continued in use until 1731. In that year Pierre Gaultier de Varennes, Sieur de la Vérendrye, learned from the Indians of three rivers leading to the "Western Sea"—the St. Louis, the Pigeon, and the Kaministiquia. Of the three, La Vérendrye chose the shortest, the Pigeon, by way of the Great Carrying Place, the Grand Portage, in extreme northeastern Minnesota. Although he did not travel the route in 1731, instead sending his nephew La Jemeraye to establish a post on Rainy Lake, he did follow it the next year, building Fort St. Charles on what is now the Northwest Angle on Lake of the Woods. From this time on, the Grand Portage route was used extensively by French and British traders until 1802–1803 when, as a result of the Treaty of Paris establishing the international boundary at the Pigeon River, the British North West Company moved its headquarters to the Kaministiquia (now Thunder Bay, Ontario).

Of all the French traders, none had a greater impact on the exploration of Canada than La Vérendrye. From Grand Portage northwestward along the border lakes, to Lake Winnipeg, and the Saskatchewan River, he and his sons established a chain of posts and gave substance to the cartography of the times. The *coureurs de bois* who preceded him, and the French traders who followed, developed a remarkable wilderness know-how and trading expertise greatly envied by the English. The French had learned well from the Indians the manner of living in the wilderness. They had adopted the Indian's dress, his canoe, snowshoes, toboggan, moccasins, and had taken Indian women as their wives, *à la façon du pays* ("in the manner of the country").

Following the defeat of the French by British forces at Quebec in 1760, British traders were quick to move into the Northwest. Men like Alexander Henry, the Frobishers, and others also realized the importance of adopting the methods of the French. They studied the routes they followed and the significance of corn, the canoe, and the French voyageur to the fur trade. Many of the French who had been involved in the trade, including the guides, interpreters, voyageurs, and others, now worked for the British out of Montreal—the "master pedlars" they were called by the English on the Bay.

When the master pedlars first entered the Northwest trade, the western terminus for the goods shipped out of Montreal was Michilimackinac. It was to this point, at the west end of Lake Huron, that the winterers brought their furs. However, with the extended lines of trade into the Northwest developed between 1765 and 1775, another transfer point was established at Grand Portage. Those who had wintered in the Northwest found it impossible to make it to Michilimackinac and return in one season. By the early 1770's, the route of the traders from Montreal and Grand Portage fell directly across the upper reaches of the main rivers flowing to the Bay, the life-lines of trade for the "Honourable Company." The results were devastating. At last, the Hudson's Bay Company, finding it difficult to get the Indians to come to the Bay posts, established Cumberland House in 1774 at a strategic location on the Saskatchewan. This signaled the English move to the interior, and the competition grew more intense.

The Montreal-based traders had, by this time, extended their lines of trade to such distances that the cost of transporting goods into the Northwest was becoming excessive. They were already on the Saskatchewan and were quickly moving west and northward. The problems of supply and provisioning were mounting. In the winter of 1775 and 1776, a number of independent traders, including Alexander Henry and Thomas Frobisher, in a move to economize, joined stock, and agreed, when the season was over, to divide the pelts and the meat. The returns of the general stock were very successful. In 1776 Thomas Frobisher, at Isle à la Crosse, met Indians from the Athabasca country where they traded twelve thousand beaver skins besides large numbers of otter and marten. In 1778 traders on the Saskatchewan pooled their stock to send Peter Pond to the Athabasca after Frobisher had met with such remarkable success. Pond, first trader to cross the 13-mile Methye Portage to gain access to the Athabasca via the Clearwater, wintered on the Athabasca River, coming out in 1779 with so many furs that it was necessary for him to return the following year for a cache he had left behind.

A major contribution of the Indian, pemmican (a mixture of meat, grease and berries) provided the food to sustain the voyageurs on their long trips into the far Northwest. Posts on the Saskatchewan—Cumberland House, Fort Vermilion, and others on both the north and south branches in the buffalo country—became known as "pemmican posts." At Cumberland House were stored huge amounts of this nutritious food to supply the canoe brigades going to and from Athabasca.

The first joining of the independent traders at Beaver Lake in 1775 has been viewed by some historians as the beginning of the North West Company. It was not, however, until 1783–1784 that the company under that name was formally organized with headquarters at Grand Portage.

To give the reader an idea of the exchange value of the beaver pelts in 1784, when the North West Company was founded, one can examine the Standard of Trade at the Hudson's Bay Company in that year: for 1 beaver the natives could obtain "2 iron hatchets or 2 [ice] Chizzels; for 12 beaver, 1 gun of four feet; and for 1½ beaver, 1 handkerchief." The standard on these items hadn't changed since 1748. [*The Beaver*, December, 1948, page 5.]

Each summer for the next twenty years Grand Portage was the scene of great activity. At times as many as a thousand men—bourgeois holding meetings, clerks busy sorting and repacking goods, winterers from the North and pork eaters from Montreal—gathered for the rendezvous. These were days of excitement—feasting, dancing, drinking, and hell raising. Great effort was expended carrying the *pieces* (two ninety-pound packs at a time) over the grueling 8½-mile portage to Fort Charlotte where they were loaded into the North canoes. At an opening known as the Meadows, a short distance upstream from Partridge Falls, the voyageurs had one last grand drinking spree.

In 1803 the North West Company, as a result of the treaty of Paris which placed Grand Portage in American territory, moved its headquarters to Kaministiquia. The XY Company followed in 1804. Alexander Henry the Younger said of his journey to the new post in 1803, "The route was more difficult with consequent complaints from the men and a smaller load (by two pieces) for the canoes." [Harold A. Innis, *The Fur Trade in Canada*, page 229.] In 1807 the Kaministiquia post was named Fort William in honor of William McGillivray, one of the most influential partners of the North West Company.

The year 1808 witnessed the formation of the American Fur Company under the already-wealthy John Jacob Astor. Eventually, after increasing pressures from the United States government, British fur interests were removed from American territory, and that country was left entirely to the Americans.

Between the years 1800 and 1820, competition between the Hudson's Bay Company and the North West Company became cut-throat and was even marked by murder. The North West Company, maintaining a string of posts almost to the Pacific and north along the Athabasca and Mackenzie rivers, found itself over-extended, with costs mounting. It had long been envious of the Hudson's Bay Company's geographical advantage with ships able to sail right into the heart of the North American continent. In July of 1805, the proprietors of the North West Company, at a meeting held at Kaministiquia, discussed the possibility of obtaining a transit for their property through Hudson Bay to the Northwest. This proposal met with no success.

Eventually the Hudson's Bay Company, with the establishment of more posts in the far Northwest, put increased pressure on its competitors and in the area where it hurt the most—the Athabasca country. Amalgamation was inevitable. On March 26, 1821, the two fur company giants—the Hudson's Bay and the North West companies—merged, thus ending a dramatic chapter in Canadian history. In the next few decades, both the Hudson's Bay and the American Fur companies expanded, the former into the Arctic and the latter into the American West. The 1830's and 40's witnessed a decline in the demand for beaver as fashions changed and the beaver hat lost its popularity. Before the middle of the nineteenth century, Hercules Dousman, American Fur Company agent at Prairie du Chien (Wisconsin), wrote gloomy letters on the state of the London fur market.

During the last half of the nineteenth century, there were continual changes in transportation methods and routes in an attempt to increase efficiency. With the move into the Arctic on the part of the Hudson's Bay Company, the Arctic white fox and the seal became important furs.

The story of the fur trade would not be complete without mention of other trading companies operating in North America, principally among them Revillon Frères. Although not active in trade on this continent until the early twentieth century, the company played a dominant role in the world fur market, and was renowned for its innovative fashion creations in fur apparel. The Revillon Frères firm had its origin in Paris with Francois Givelet, one of 214 fur traders operating there in 1723. From meager beginnings, it expanded to a world-wide business, buying exotic furs from every section of the globe including Siberia, Africa, and Afghanistan. Today its operations include not only fur but industry, financial activities, perfume, and real estate, with offices in every major city of the world.

After the fur trade opened the country, settlement followed. As the process of interaction with the native populations advanced, the nature of trade inventories changed, as did the image of the Hudson's Bay Company. From a company built on remote fur posts came one of huge retail stores in the major Canadian cities. The small red-and-white company stores, however, are still evident in the settlements across the North, and the buying of furs continues as does extending credit to the Indian and Inuit. The Hudson's Bay Company, as with other major stores, now issues credit cards to all customers.

Now in the small HBC stores are stereo recorders, television sets, down jackets, blue jeans, outboard motors, snowmobiles, soft drinks, fresh fruits, and vegetables. Many of the remote settlements today are served by aircraft, but some still depend on the annual ships to bring in the heavier supplies like oil, lumber, etc. In the 1970's I witnessed an Inuit woman buying a slice of watermelon in a Hudson's Bay store at Pond Inlet, 500 miles north of the Arctic Circle! The business in furs today represents only a very small percentage of the sales of the Hudson's Bay Company, but its commerce in furs continues. The company has the honor of being the oldest business firm in continuous operation on the North American continent. While the copper kettles and muskrat spears are gone from the shelves, a few of the trade items remain—namely the famous Hudson's Bay point blankets, duffle, calico, beads, ice chisels and the crooked knives.

In the American West, the mountain men are gone, but in many areas of the United States farm boys and others continue to trap muskrats, mink, fox, opossum, and raccoon. In some of the northern states, the trappers are bringing in beaver, otter, fisher, fox, and mink which are sold to a local fur buyer. In the Canadian provinces, many of the trappers still manage a fair standard of living.

While the frontiers of the fur trade and its cast of characters have faded, they remain vividly in the minds of those of us who seek high adventure from an exciting chapter in North American history. For both Canada and the United States, the fur trade remains an important part of our heritage.

The Demand

"Axes, knives, mere nails, being of tempered iron, made
stone hatchets and bone needles and awls antediluvian. An
unbreakable, unburnable iron or brass kettle wiped out at a
stroke all the labour and care incidental to a whole series
of wooden, bark or even pottery vessels." [John Bartlet
Brebner, *Explorers of North America,*
1492–1806, page 115.]

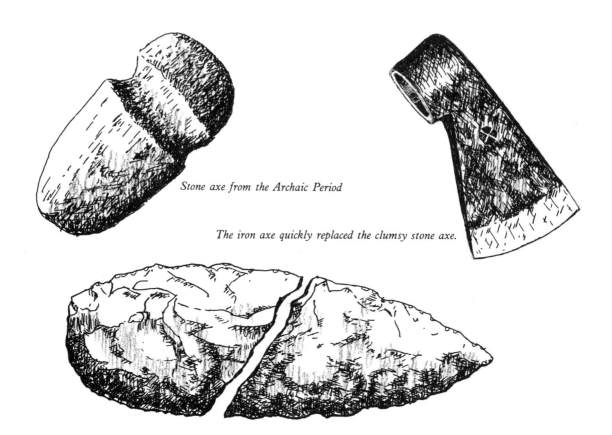

Stone axe from the Archaic Period

The iron axe quickly replaced the clumsy stone axe.

Flint knife from the Woodland Period found at Crane Lake, Minnesota, by Kristi Wheeler Duckwall. Each half was found in two different years and a dozen feet apart. Length, 3½ inches.

TOOLS

When the European set foot on the North American continent, the natives were still in the Stone Age. All of their tools for chopping, cutting, pounding, drilling, fishing, sewing, and hunting, except for some fashioned from native copper, were of stone, wood or bone. Weapons for warring on other tribes were of these same materials. One can only imagine their utter amazement on first seeing objects of iron, copper, and brass.

"Axes and hatchets were made of some form of iron, either wrought iron or steel. The wrought iron tended to be brittle and to break easily under a heavy blow, but it was cheap. Steel axes, on the other hand, were too expensive for ordinary use, but this problem was solved by inserting a narrow strip of steel for a bit." [Kenneth Kidd and Marie Gérin Lajoie, "Montreal Merchants' Records," 1708–1775, mimeographed.]

"Hatchets, knives, scissors, needles, and a steel to strike fire with. These instruments are now common among the Indians. They all take these instruments from the Europeans and reckon the hatchets and knives much better than those which they formerly made of stones and bones. The stone hatchets of the ancient Indians are very rare in Canada." [Peter Kalm, *Travels into North America: The America of 1750*, Vol. II, quoted in Harold A. Innis, *The Fur Trade in Canada*, page 110.]

COOKING UTENSILS

With cooking utensils also, the Indians were limited to the materials found in their environment. Clay pots and bark vessels were used for cooking, storage, and agriculture. Spoons, ladles, and scrapers were made of wood, bone or horn.

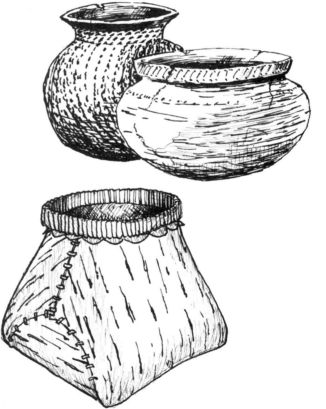

Copper trade kettles, introduced by the European, eventually replaced the clay pots. Some of the earliest French kettles had three legs and were made of heavy iron. These were never popular with the natives who were frequently on the move.

Some containers were made by northern woodland Indians from birch bark: trays and baskets for serving food, storing wild rice, maple sugar, catching sap, gathering berries and fruit; and watertight vessels for cooking. Water was often heated by dropping hot stones into a bark vessel like that illustrated here.

FUR FASHIONS IN EUROPE

1678

1779

1827

The Beaver Hat

The fashions of Europe determined the demand for fur. The marten or sable was one of the most sought-after furs, and, in the earliest days of the trade, was worn only by princes and great lords, but, of all the furs hunted across North America, the beaver was by far the most important. According to Arthur S. Morton in his *A History of the Canadian West to 1870–71*, page 22:

"At the outset there was no special demand for beaver in Europe, not until the hat-makers realized its value for their craft . . . Beaver hats became the rage, and the value of beaver fur was enhanced accordingly. The traffic in fur now began in earnest." In the nineteenth century, when fashions changed and the beaver hat went out of style, the fur trade steadily declined.

The Barterers

"To be successfully prosecuted, the fur trade required
the cooperation of both parties. In the broadest sense, it was
a partnership for the exploitation of resources."
[Arthur J. Ray, *Indians in the Fur Trade: their role as
hunters, trappers and middlemen in the lands southwest of
Hudson Bay, 1660–1870*, page xi.]

NATIVE AMERICANS

The Indian men and women illustrated are dressed in costumes reflecting the change from leather to cloth. The trade blanket was almost universally adopted by the Indian and worn in a variety of ways. [Illustrations based on sketches and paintings done in the early nineteenth century by Peter Rindisbacher and George Catlin.]

The North American fur trade could not have existed without the Indian who not only caught the fur-bearing animals but provided a ready market for the white man's goods and showed him how to exist in a harsh environment. The Indian provided the trader with the bark canoe, his moccasins, the snowshoe, the toboggan, and food such as wild rice, maple sugar, corn—all necessary to travel and survival. In most cases it was the Indian who guided the European through the uncharted wilderness.

Historians in recent years are beginning to appreciate the important role of the Indian in the fur trade and to record the considerable contributions of Indian women who helped to build canoes, make snowshoes, gather and process oats (wild rice), chop wood, and work in the corn fields; made canoe sails, clothes, and moccasins; skinned and dressed fur, tanned hides, snared rabbits and martens; made maple sugar and pemmican, picked berries, smoked meat, picked ducks and geese, and netted fish. In addition to these exhausting duties, they also acted as guides and interpreters. Perhaps most importantly, the Indian women often served a political function as the liaison between Indian and trader.

BOURGEOIS, MERCHANT, AND CLERK

It has been said that it takes two to bargain, and the same is true to barter. The Indian in the fur trade was primarily the gatherer of furs. The European or white man, on the other hand, was the provider of the goods—kettles, knives, guns, cloth, beads, hatchets, etc. Not all the Europeans who were engaged in the fur trade did the actual bartering. This was primarily done by the trader, usually that person who was in charge of the post where the barter took place. Often referred to as the bourgeois, the partner or the trader had charge of one or several posts in the interior and was actively engaged in trading during the winter. In addition to the bourgeois or trader, there was the agent or merchant in Montreal who did the purchasing, packing, and forwarding of trade goods, provisions, and liquor as well as the hiring of the *engagés* or voyageurs. The merchant also ordered the freight canoes from the canoe factory in Trois Rivières.

Another important participant in the trade was the clerk, usually a young man apprenticed to the trade for up to seven years. It was a position which often led to a partnership, a considerable advancement. The clerk's duties included keeping journals, supervising trade, settling accounts, packing furs, and making trade goods up into bales or "*pieces.*" The bourgeois, merchant, and clerk were literate, whereas the French Canadian voyageur was almost always illiterate, signing his engagements or contracts with an X.

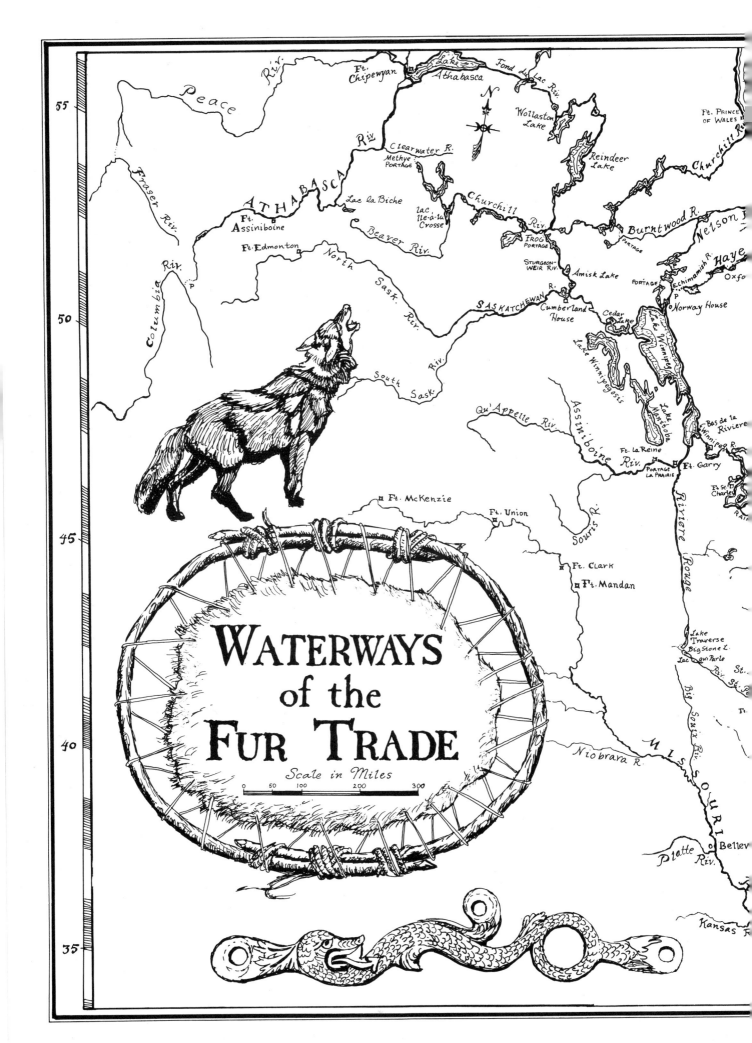

HUDSON

BAY

York Factory

Knee Lake
Lake

RIV.

SEVERN RIV.

JAMES

BAY

Ft.
GEORGE

ALBANY
Ft.

MOOSE Riv.

CHARLES
Ft.

MOOSE Riv.

ALBANY RIVER

lac St. Joseph

PORTAGE

PORTAGE

ENGLISH R.

lac Nipigon

Missinatbi R.

Abittibi R.

Lake of the
Woods

Rainy Lake

Ft. St.
Pierre

Namakan
Lake La Croix
Vermilion
PORTAGE RIV.

KAMINISTIKWIA RIVER

PIDGEON
RIV.

Ft. WILLIAM

GRAND
PORTAGE

Lac
à la Pointe

Superior

St. Mary's Falls

Sault Ste. Marie

PORTAGE

Mattawa Riv.

Riv. Utawas
(Ottawa Riv.)

Trois Rivieres

Quebec

LAWRENCE

Montreal

Lachine

Riv. St.

French
River

lac Nipissing

SAVANAH
PORTAGE

St. LOUIS RIV.

Boi
Brule
R.

PORTAGE

KETTLE
R.

Lac Court
Oreilles

SERPENT
R.

St. CROIX RIV.

Ouiscousin Riv.

Green
Bay

Mackinac Is.

Ft.
Michilimack-
inac

Lake Huron

Lake
St. Clair

Ft.
Frontenac

Ft.
Ticonderoga

Lake Ontario

Portage

Mohawk R.
Albany

Ft.
Stanwix

Ft. Niagra

Hudson Riv.

Anthony's
Falls

Fort Beauharnois

Chippeway Riv.

MISSISSIPPI

Lake Pepin

TREMPEALEAU

"Huillier"

Fox Riv.

Missini

Lake Michigan

Prairie
du Chien

PORTAGE

Fox Plains R.

Chicago R.

MISSION
St. Joseph's Riv.

Ft. St.
Joseph

Ft. Pontchartrain
du Detroit

Lake Erie

Maumee R.

Allegheny

PORTAGE

Ft. Venango

New York

Philadelphia

des Moines Riv.

Illinois Riv.

Kankakee
Riv.

P
Ft.
St. Joseph

Ft. St. Louis

Ouabache RIV.

Ft. St. Louis
(Crèvecoeur)

Ft. des Miamis

Ft. Sandusky

Ft. Duquesne

PORTAGE

Williamsburg

RIVER

Ft. Orleans

Cahokia

KASKASKIAS (ST. LOUIS)

Ft. Chartres

KASKASKIA

Ft. Massiac

VINCENNES

Ft. Ouiatenon

Ohio River

Falls of the Ohio

55

50

45

40

35

DPC '84

The Transporting

"The elaborate transportation system necessary to carry
on the trade from Grand Portage to the interior and to the
Athabasca required a highly developed organization for the
supply of provisions. . . . The difficulty of carrying large
supplies of provisions in canoes led to the establishment
of provision depots . . . " [Harold A. Innis, *The Fur
Trade in Canada*, pages 231, 232.]

CANOES OF THE FUR TRADE

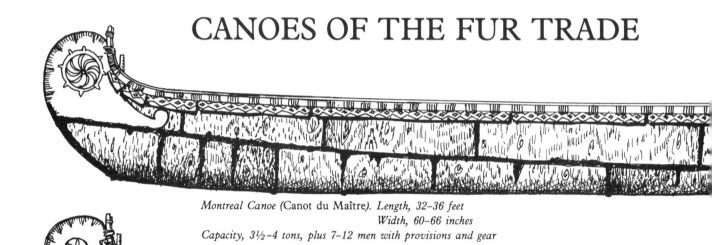

Montreal Canoe (Canot du Maître). Length, 32–36 feet
Width, 60–66 inches
Capacity, 3½–4 tons, plus 7–12 men with provisions and gear

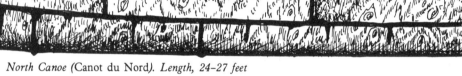

North Canoe (Canot du Nord). Length, 24–27 feet
Width, 50–60 inches.
Capacity, 1½ tons, plus 4–6 men with provisions and gear

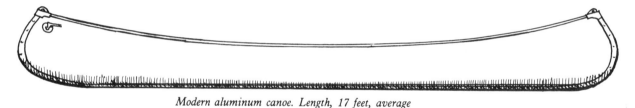

Modern aluminum canoe. Length, 17 feet, average

Ojibwa Canoe. Length, 15–16 feet

Of the many contributions, with the exception of furs, the Indians made to the fur trade—the snowshoe, the moccasin, the toboggan, pemmican, and the birch-bark canoe—the canoe was, without question, the most important. History tells us that the first French to build bark canoes learned the art from the Algonquin, the original canoe builders. [Edwin T. Adney and Howard I. Chapelle, *The Bark Canoes and Skin Boats of North America*, page 135. Kenneth G. Roberts and Philip Shackleton, *The Canoe*, page 173.]

During the eighteenth century, many of the largest canoes, the "*maître canots*," were built at Trois Rivières near Montreal. The North West Company, through its merchants, found it necessary to order canoes. These were made not only at Trois Rivières but at such western locations as St. Joseph's Island, Grand Portage (later Fort William), and at Rainy Lake. According to Adney and Chapelle in *The Bark Canoes and Skin Boats of North America*, page 138, "Each 'canoe road' forming the main lines of travel . . . had requirements that effected the size of the canoes employed on it." The Montreal canoe was used on the Montreal-Great Lakes route. At the western end of this route, a smaller craft, the North canoe, was used on the long trip into the North-

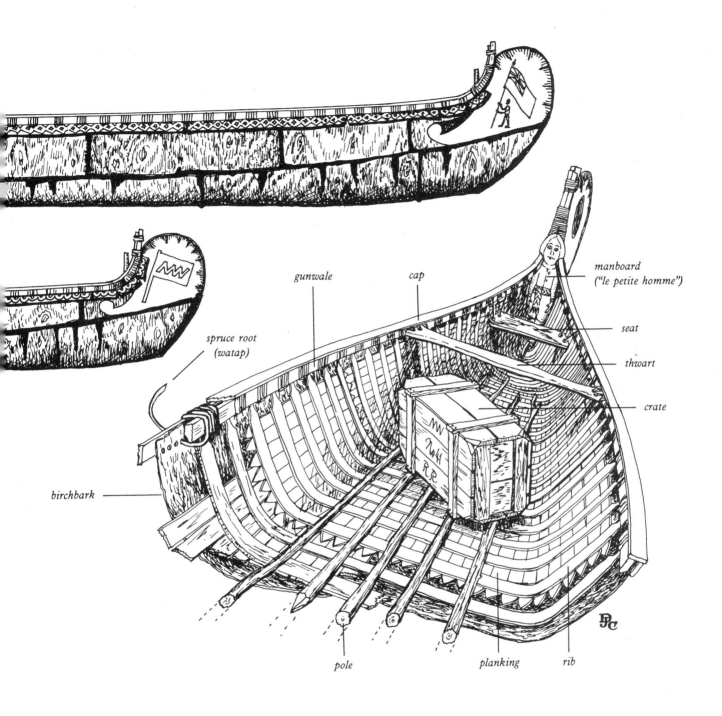

gunwale

cap

manboard
("le petite homme")

spruce root
(watap)

seat

thwart

crate

birchbark

pole

planking

rib

west. Marie Gérin-Lajoie, in her translation of the "Montreal Merchants' Records, 1708–75," reports: "Nowhere are linear measures mentioned in reference to canoes; their size is always indicated in terms of 'places,' a term presumably adopted from the native people's figurative language. It is possible that they found this term more appropriate since there apparently were no specific sizes until, perhaps, the advent of the famous *canot du maître*." The term "places" did not mean places for people, but rather spaces between thwarts or crossbars. The largest canoes mentioned by the French merchants were eight-place canoes, whereas the smaller

models were four or six places. Reference to sizes in French or English measure came only when traders and travelers began observing the characteristics of the canoes and began writing about them.

Nicholas Garry, in his *Diary of Nicholas Garry*, page 118, wrote: "We now travel in two Canoes Mr. Bird accompanying me and Mr. McRobb a clerk of the North West Company and Mr. McGillivray. Our Canoes are much smaller than the Montreal Canoe and are called the 'North Canoes' which Designation 'North Men' is given to the Men who from long Experience and being more inured to the Changes of Climate and Fatigue and

Privations are more hardy. Our Canoe is about 25 Feet in Length by about 4½ Feet in Breadth and weighing about 2½ cwt [280 pounds, English weight]."

"We witnessed the whole Process of Loading one of the Canoes. The first Part of the Loading is to place 4 Poles or long Sticks at the bottom of the Canoe which run the whole Length. These support the whole weight and prevent the Bottom being injured. The Pieces or Packs which weigh about 90 lbs. each are then placed in the Canoe and with wonderful precision, each Piece seeming to fit. The most weighty Goods are put at the Bottom, the Provisions, Cooking Utensils, Liqur &C., are likewise put in; at the Bow is placed a large Roll of Bark in case of Accident, with a supply of Wattape, Gum &C." [*Diary of Nicholas Garry*, page 90.]

Throughout the fur-trade literature, references to amounts of lading or cargo placed in the canoes varied according to canoe size and the nature of the routes over which the craft was to travel. For example, the Montreal canoes from La Chine to the eastern end of Lake Superior carried the standard load, but to make the difficult trip on Lake Superior to Grand Portage or Fort William a few pieces were removed. On the Kaministiquia, which was a more shallow route, fewer pieces were carried. The usual cargo of one Montreal canoe was, besides eight or ten men's personal baggage, "sixty-five packages of goods, six hundred weight of biscuit, two hundred weight of port, three bushels of pease, for the

men's provision; two oil-cloths to cover the goods, a sail, etc., an axe, a towing-line . . ." [Archibald McDonald, *Peace River. A Canoe Voyage from Hudson's Bay to the Pacific*, as quoted in Edwin C. Guillet, *Pioneer Travel in Upper Canada*, pages 31–32.] The above cargo amounted to over four tons. For the North canoe, a smaller craft, the weight was considerably less, about 1½ tons.

Alexander Henry the Elder describes a most interesting procedure he followed when he wintered at Amisk (Beaver) Lake in 1775 with a party numbering forty-three. "Our canoes were disposed of on scaffolds; for the ground being frozen, we could not bury them as is the usual practice, and which is done to protect them from the severity of cold which occasions the bark to contract and split." [Alexander Henry, *Travels and Adventures in Canada and the Indian Territories Between the Years 1760 and 1776*, pages 264–265.]

This method of protecting the bark canoes from damage in the northern winters was not new to the traders. "They [the Ojibwa] made canoes of birch bark reinforced with the gum of spruce or pine, and in these navigated the Great Lakes and tributaries in the summertime. For winter they buried their canoes so that they would not snap in the intense cold." [Eleanor Burke Leacock and Nancy Oestreich Lurie, eds., *North American Indians in Historical Perspective*, page 169.]

LE PETITE HOMME

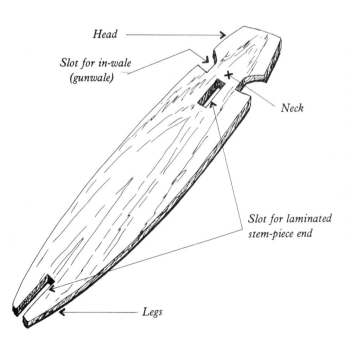

Head

Slot for in-wale (gunwale)

Neck

Slot for laminated stem-piece end

Legs

Le Petite Homme (manboard). "In the old French canoes and in those of the North West Company, the board was carved or painted to represent a human figure, *le petite homme*, which was often made in the likeness of a voyageur in his best clothes." [Edwin Adney and Howard I. Chapelle, *The Bark Canoes and Skin Boats of North America*, page 150.]

"*Le petite homme*, or manboard, so-called because of its shape, looking much like a distorted man, was a functional part of the birch-bark canoe. Its purpose was to form a support for the stem piece, to provide a support base for the gunwales, to give strength to each end of the canoe, to secure the cedar sheathing at each end, to help define the curvature of the canoe nose (both ends), and to complete a finished look on each inside end. The manboard is called 'wanakonjaa' in the Ojibwe language . . . As the fur trade became competitive, the companies developed fanciful designs and logos that graced the ends of their canoes. The Frenchmen quickly took advantage of the manboards' shape and decorated it as a 'self portrait,' an imprint of his trade . . . There is no known case where the Indian used the shape of the manboard coupled with drawn design to purposely represent a human figure such as found in fur-trade canoes." [Letter, May 18, 1983, to the author from Earl Nyholm, assistant professor of Ojibwe, Bemidji State University.]

LES VOYAGEURS

Guide

Winterer

Porkeater

The French Canadian voyageur has taken his place in North American history with the sailor, cowboy, and lumberjack. In the last decade especially, there has been a phenomenal interest in this little-understood figure from the eighteenth and early nineteenth centuries. As with other heroes of the past, the voyageurs have taken on an aura of more fiction than fact. Some historians have described the voyageur as a picturesque romantic—a free spirit, singing, packing, and happily paddling along the wilderness rivers and lakes.

There is no question that the voyageur played a significant role in the early history of North America and particularly that of the fur trade. Known to the fur traders as an "*engagé*," he was an employee engaged for a specified time, for an agreed-upon wage, and with specific duties. In general the voyageur was hired to paddle a canoe and carry cargo over portages, and nothing more. One might call him an eighteenth-century truck driver or longshoreman. His contemporaries who described the voyageur were either fur traders, who often took a jaundiced view, or travelers and others encountering him, who pictured him more romantically. The description by Edwin T. Adney and Howard I. Chapelle in *The Bark Canoes and Skin Boats of North America*, page 143, is, no doubt, a more accurate one: "The traditional picture of the fur-trade voyageur as a happy, carefree adventurer was hardly a true one, at least in the 19th century. With poor food hastily prepared, back-breaking loads, and continual exposure, his lot was a very hard one at best. The monstrous packs usually brought physical injury, and the working life of a packer was very short." It is true that the voyageur, in an earlier day, was permitted some trading to add to his meager existence, but the mosquitoes, the mire on the portages, the cold water, the constant dangers on the rivers and lakes, and the frequent injuries on the portages were the same and made his lot hard and not to be envied.

To provide the reader an opportunity to make a personal assessment, following are a few descriptions of the voyageur by his contemporaries: "As voyageurs, or ramblers of any kind, they find much delight, so that a number of them be together. They will endure privations with great patience; will live on peas and Indian corn for years together. . . . They are good at composing easy, extemporaneous songs, somewhat smutty, but never intolerant. Many of their canoe songs are exquisite, more particularly the air they give them. . . . We must be in a canoe with a dozen hearty paddlers, the lake pure, the weather fine, and the rapids past, before their influence can be particularly felt. Music and song I have revelled in all of my life, and must own that the *chanson de voyageur* has delighted me above all others, excepting those of Scotland." [John Mactaggart, *Three Years in Canada*, 1829, quoted in Edwin C. Guillet, *Pioneer Travel in Upper Canada*, page 23.]

A further portrayal follows: "Possibly Auld [superintendent of the Hudson's Bay Company's Northern Department] over-estimates the amount of control which the church has over the French Canadians [voyageurs] for, although they come from devout families, most of them set aside their religion when they enter the Northwest. They are usually young when they come and, because they are generally illiterate, they tend to forget the little religion they ever had when there is no church to remind them of it, so that, after many years in the country, they do not seem to observe the Sabbath (or any manner of worship) any more than do the savages themselves." [Eric Ross, *Beyond the River and the Bay*, page 23.]

"The Canadians [voyageurs] are chosen Men inured to hardships & fatigue, under which most of Your [Hudson's Bay Company] Present Servants would sink, a Man in the Canadian Service who cannot carry two Packs of eighty Lbs. each, one & a half League losses [loses] his trip that is his Wages." [W. Stewart Wallace, ed., *Documents Relating to the North West Company*, page 43.]

Daniel Williams Harmon, fur trader, in *A Journal of Voyages and Travels in the Interior of North America*, pages 235-236, gives us his impressions of the Canadian voyageurs: "They are not brave; but when they apprehend little danger, they will often, as they say, play the man. They are very deceitful, and exceedingly smooth and polite, and are even gross flatterers to the face of a person, whom they will basely slander, behind his back. They pay little regard to veracity or to honesty. Their word is not to be trusted; and they are much addicted to pilfering, and will even steal articles of considerable value, when a favourable opportunity offers. A secret they cannot keep. They rarely feel gratitude, though they are often generous. They are obedient, but not faithful servants. By flattering their vanity, of which they have not a little, they may be persuaded to undertake the most difficult enterprises, provided their lives are not endangered. Although they are generally unable to read, yet they acquire considerable knowledge of human nature, and some general information, in regard to the state of this country. As they leave Canada while they are young, they have but little knowledge of the principles of the religion, which their Priests profess to follow, and before they have been long in the Indian country, they pay little more attention to the sabbath, or the worship of God, or any other Divine institution, than the savages themselves . . . all their chat is about horses, dogs, canoes, women and strong men, who can fight a good battle."

The Hudson's Bay Company had its problems as the following indicates: "Even when canoes were obtainable, canoemen were not; and for long the Company [Hudson's Bay] was forced to rely on the unpredictable results of hiring Indians to work the canoes. It possessed no equivalent of the Canadian voyageurs, 'those natural water Dogs,' as a later Company servant described them, who handled the light but capacious *canot du nord* with consummate skill." [*The Beaver*, Autumn, 1970, page 31.]

An excerpt from the *Diary of Nicholas Garry*, page 100, illustrates the humor of the voyageur: "We then embarked on a small Lake not 50 yards in Breadth, a Sort of Basin with high Lands on all sides, at the End a small channel the sides of the Canoe touching the Banks. Here they have a standing Joke against a Voyageur who They say was stopped in this little Bowl by a Head Wind."

CANOE PADDLES

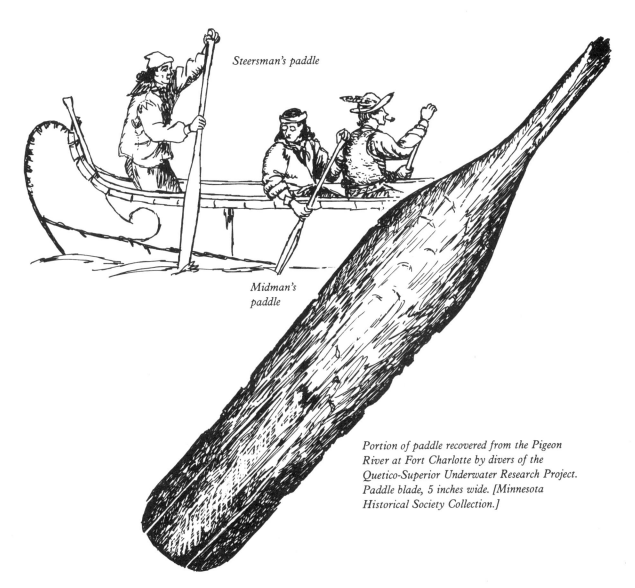

Steersman's paddle

Midman's paddle

Portion of paddle recovered from the Pigeon River at Fort Charlotte by divers of the Quetico-Superior Underwater Research Project. Paddle blade, 5 inches wide. [Minnesota Historical Society Collection.]

"Many of the voyageurs showed their characteristic love of bright colours by staining them a vivid vermilion." [Edwin C. Guillet, *Pioneer Travel in Upper Canada*, page 42.]

"The voyageur was particular about his paddle; no man in his right mind would use a blade wider than between 4½ and 5 inches, for anything wider would exhaust him in a short distance. The paddle reached to about the user's chin, when he stood with the tip of the paddle on the ground in front of him. Longer paddles, about 6 feet long, were used by the bow and stern men, the two most skillful voyageurs in the canoe and the highest paid. These men had, also, spare paddles whose total length was eight feet or more; these were used in running rapids only . . . The blades were sometimes painted white, the tips in some color such as red, blue, green or black. . . . " [Edwin T. Adney and Howard I. Chapelle, *The Bark Canoes and Skin Boats of North America*, page 152.]

"When on bad rapids I repeatedly saw our guide turn our canoe aside in less than a second, by a stroke of his big paddle, when detecting a sunken rock within two or three feet of the bow, and that, too, when he knew that within several seconds after he must pass in dangerous proximity to other rocks, to strike one of which would insure us a wetting, if not worse." ["Diary of Robert Kennicott," quoted in Chicago Academy of Sciences, *Transactions*, Vol. 1, part 2, page 159.]

CANOE SAILS

Wooden toggles, used to raise and lower sails, were found underwater at Fort Charlotte at the western end of the Grand Portage. [Minnesota Historical Society Collection.]

The French adopted the Indian's bark canoe and certainly his use of the sail. With thousands of miles of lake travel facing the traders, the sail offered a welcome respite to weary voyageurs. Its use, however, was not without danger. "The use of sail by the Micmacs [Indians] was reported in very early French narratives, although it was very likely a borrowed idea." [Kenneth G. Roberts and Philip Shackleton, *The Canoe*, page 168.]

Few historians, and even those with some knowledge of the fur trade, are aware of the extent to which the sail was used on the fur-trade canoes. Sails on the canoes were constructed so as to allow them to be raised or lowered depending on the velocity of the wind. To lower was to "reef" the sail. "We reefed our sail down to two feet, and even that was more than the canoe could carry with safety." [*The Manuscript Journals of Alexander Henry and David Thompson, 1799–1814*, Vol. II, page 467.]

The use of the sail on large bodies of water was tempting and often resulted in tragic accidents as the following illustrates: "October 1778 . . . the Indian. . . informs me he was 12 days Weather bound in the Sea Lake [Lake Winnipeg], which is the cause of his late arrival . . . he says they lost two canoes, one on the Great Fall and another in crossing Cedar Lake by carrying too much sail, the men was saved but no goods." [*Cumberland and Hudson House Journals, 1775–82*, First Series, page 265.] Many sailing accidents involved loss of life. Of all the large lakes, Winnipeg and Superior were among the worst.

CANOES ON THE PORTAGE

Figure 2

Figure 1

The birch-bark canoes of the fur traders were loaded and unloaded in the water to prevent damage to the fragile craft. In portaging the six-fathom or Montreal canoes (Figure 1), they were carried bottom-side-up by four to six men, depending on the difficulty of the terrain. The smaller North canoes (Figure 2) were carried bottom-side-down on the shoulders of two and at times three men. The lead man tied a rope to the bow to hold the canoe in position as he held his end of the canoe.

"When arrived at a portage, the bowman instantly jumps in the water, to prevent the canoe from touching the bottom, while the others tie their slings to the packages in the canoe and swing them on their backs to carry over the portage. The bowman and steersman carry their [North] canoe, a duty from which the middlemen are exempt." [L.R. Masson, *Les Bourgeois de la Campagnie du Nord-Ouest*, page 313.]

"The manner of carrying the [Montreal] Canoe: She is first turned over. Four men then go into the water, two at each End, raise the Canoe and then two more place themselves about midships of the Gunwale on the opposite side." [*Diary of Nicholas Garry*, page 96.]

GRAND PORTAGE VS. THE KAMINISTIQUIA

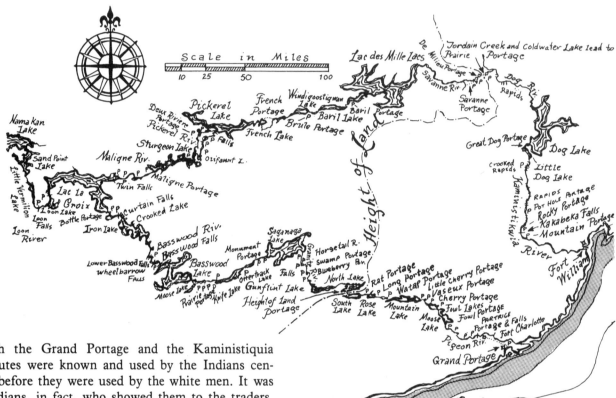

Both the Grand Portage and the Kaministiquia routes were known and used by the Indians centuries before they were used by the white men. It was the Indians, in fact, who showed them to the traders. Routes were often referred to as "roads" by the fur traders.

The route to Lac la Pluie or Rainy Lake by way of the Kaministiquia was first used by Jacques de Noyon about the year 1688. From that time on until 1731, this was the way the French *couriers des bois* traveled to the country northwest of Lake Superior. In the late 1720's, the French explorer-fur trader, Pierre La Vérendrye, began asking local Indians about the best route to the great river. "I acquainted myself with the route through different savages, who all made the same statement, that there are three routes or rivers which lead to the great river of the West. Consequently I had a map made of these three rivers, in order that I might be able to choose the shortest and easiest road. I had the honour, Monsieur, of sending you that map as it was traced for me by Auchagah, showing the three rivers which flow into Lake Superior, namely the one called Fond du Lac river [the St. Louis], the Nantouagan [Pigeon] and the Kaministiquia. The two latter are those on which everything is marked with exactness on the map, lakes, rapids, portages, the side on which the portage must be made, and the heights of land; all this is represented or indicated. Comparing these two routes, the river Nantouagan, which is two days' journey from the river Kaministiquia going toward the extremity of the lake, is,

it seems to me, the one to be preferred. It has, it is true, forty-two portages, while the Kaministiquia has only twenty-two; but, on the other hand, it has no rapids, while the other has twelve, two of which are long and very shallow. Besides, the road is straight and one third shorter." [*Journals and Letters of Pierre Gaultier de Varennes, Sieur de La Vérendrye, and His Sons*, pages 52–55.]

La Vérendrye's men used the Pigeon route in 1731 to build a post on Rainy Lake. From that year on, it was used by the French and later by the Scotch and English traders until 1803, when the North West Company moved its headquarters to the Kaministiquia. Before the United States-Canadian boundary was finally established, the Americans argued that the "common water route" was the Kaministiquia, while the Canadians argued it was the St. Louis River. The Pigeon was the final choice.

Note: One of the best descriptions of the Kaministiquia route is given in the diary of Robert Kennicott, who made the trip in a North canoe, in 1859. [Chicago Academy of Sciences, *Transactions*, Vol. 1, part 2, pages 146–155.]

PIECES ON THE PORTAGE

Most of the routes used by the fur traders were by water via a marvelous network of rivers and lakes. Along these hundreds and even thousands of miles of water were places where it was necessary to carry the cargo around waterfalls, dangerous rapids, and across heights of land or watersheds. At times only the cargo had to be carried and at others the canoe also. There were places, too, where only a half or a portion of the cargo had to be portaged. This was known as a "demi-charge." Portages varied in length from a lift-over of a few feet to a portage of thirteen miles or even longer.

"The loading, made up into packages of about ninety pounds each, was carried by the men upon their backs, supported by a strap passing across the forehead. A full load is two pieces, or one hundred and eighty pounds." ["Diary of Robert Kennicott," quoted in Chicago Academy of Sciences, *Transactions*, Vol. 1, part 2, page 150.] There were instances recorded where voyageurs were known to have carried three or more pieces.

Webster's definition of a portage is "a carrying or transporting of boats and supplies overland between navigable rivers, lakes, etc., as during a canoe trip." It is certain that fur traders, and particularly voyageurs, had other definitions. There were some portages which were extremely difficult, like the Savanna Portage. During the days of the fur trade, it was one of the most important avenues of communication between the upper Mississippi Valley and the Great Lakes, according to the journals of traders, travelers, and missionaries who penetrated the region between 1760 and 1850. Specifically the route lay between Fond du Lac (Superior) to Lac des Sables (Sandy Lake) where it flows into the Mississippi River. Joseph G. Norwood, a geologist in the service of the United States government, who made a survey of this portion of Minnesota in 1848, describes the six-mile portage: " . . . The east end of the portage, for the distance of a mile and a half, runs through a tamerack swamp, which was flooded with water, and next to impassable. It is generally considered the worst 'carrying place' in the Northwest, and, judging from the great number of canoes which lie decaying along this part of it, having been abandoned in consequence of the difficulty experienced in getting them over, its reputation is well deserved." [Irving H. Hart, "The Old Savanna Portage," *Minnesota History*, June, 1927, page 128.]

Reverend William T. Boutwell, a Congregational missionary to the Indians, and a member of the Schoolcraft expedition, wrote in his diary a colorful description of the portage, from which the following is taken: "River Savannah. June 30, 1832. . . . To describe the difficulties of this portage, would puzzle a Scott, or a Knickerbocker, even. Neither language nor pencil can paint them . . . The musketoes came in hordes and threatened to carry a man alive, our [or] devour him ere they could get him away. . . . July 2, 1832. . . . The rain . . . has rendered the portage almost impassable for man or beast. The mud, for the greater part of the way will average ankle deep and from that upwards. In spots, it is difficult to find bottom—a perfect quagmire. Our men look like renegades, covered with mud from head to foot, some have lost one leg of the pantaloons, others both. Their shirts and mocassins are of a piece, full of rents and mud. Face, hands and necks, look like men scarred with the small pox." [Irving H. Hart, "The Old Savanna Portage," *Minnesota History*, June, 1927, pages 125–126.]

BATEAUX AND DUGOUTS

Birch-bark canoes were not the only watercraft used by the fur traders. In areas where there were no birch trees, canoes were constructed of hickory and elm bark, moose hide, and buffalo skin. There were also the wooden dugouts or *pirogues*, commonly used in areas of no suitable bark. These have been found in recent years in shallow lakes which have been drained. The dugout illustrated on this page is adapted from a sketch, "Kaposia to St. Paul in a Dugout," by Frank B. Mayer, the original of which is in the Newberry Library, Chicago, Illinois.

The bateaux used by the early French and English were constructed of planks. They were sharp at both ends and had straight, flaring sides with a flat bottom.

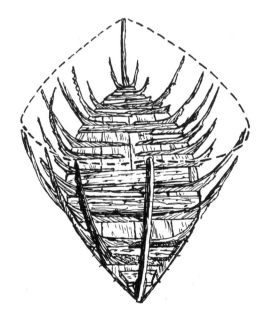

The remains of a colonial bateau salvaged by divers from Lake George, New York, in the early 1960's. [Adirondack Museum collection.]

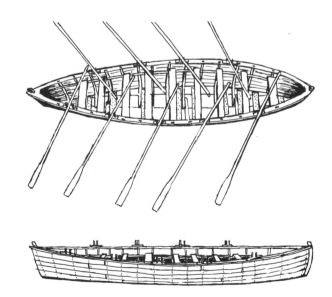

A model of the Lake George bateau constructed by John Gardner, Mystic Seaport Museum. [Model exhibited at the Adirondack Museum, Blue Mountain Lake, New York.]

TOBOGGANS AND CARIOLES

Figure 1

Figure 2

Figure 1 Toboggan scene adapted from "The Fur Trader," an anonymous portrait of John Budden, Esq., ca. 1855. [From an original work in the Glenbow Museum, Calgary, Alberta, Canada.]

Figure 2 The cariole illustrated in the foreground was used by Dr. John Rae of the Hudson's Bay Company on his trip to St. Paul from Pembina in February, 1852, by dog team. Overall length, 9 feet, 2 inches. Width at widest point, 22 inches. [Original in the Minnesota Historical Society.]

The European penetration of Canada would have been slow indeed without the Indian. Among his many contributions to the fur trade was the toboggan, used for winter travel in the north.

"A toboggan differs from a sled in that it has no runners under it, but is merely three or four thin boards lashed side by side with their front ends turned up so as to lead easily over the snow." [Douglas Leechman, *Native Tribes of Canada*, page 36.]

"January 17th [1806] Employed in making sleds, or *traineaux de glace* [toboggans], after the manner of the country." [*The Expeditions of Zebulon M. Pike*, Vol. I, page 141.]

"The cariole is intended for carrying one person only; it is a thin flat board, about eighteen inches wide, bent up in front, with a straight back behind to lean against; the sides are made of green buffalo hide, with the hair scraped completely off and dried, resembling thick parchment; this entirely covers the front part, so that a person slips into it as into a tin bath." [Paul Kane, *Wanderings of an Artist*, page 271.]

"The North West Company also makes use of a Canadian sledge called a *carriole* which is likewise drawn by either horses or dogs, depending upon the condition of the snow." [Eric Ross, *Beyond the River and the Bay*, page 73.]

THE YORK BOAT

The York boat, an innovation of the Hudson's Bay
Company, had its real origin in the Orkney Islands, the source of much of the Company's labor supply. Like the canoes of the French and the Nor'westers,
they were built in several sizes. Artist Paul Kane in 1846
writes: "These boats are about twenty-eight feet long,
and strongly built, so as to be able to stand a heavy press
of sail and rough weather, which they often encounter
in the lakes: they carry about eighty or ninety packs of
90 lbs. each, and have a crew of seven men, a steersman
and six rowers." [Paul Kane, *Wanderings of an Artist*,
page 72.]

In an article entitled "York Boats" appearing in the
Hudson's Bay Company magazine, *The Beaver*, March,
1949, page 22, R. Glover writes: "Whereas the boats
built in the 1820's had a keel length of 24–27 feet, those
on the Saskatchewan in 1858 had a keel length of 30
feet, with an overall length of 42 feet, beam 9 feet, inside
depth 3 feet. When loaded with 70 pieces they drew
only two feet of water."

As for the origin of the York boat in North America,
the HBC factor at Albany, Joseph Isbister, an Orkney-
man, in his journal for 1745, complained, "theres no
eand to building Cannoes" and expressed the intention
"to make triell to build a boat to Drawe as letle watter
as a Canno and Carie more goods." [*The Beaver*, March,
1949, page 19.] Philip Turnor, surveyor for the Hudson's Bay Company, found the boats the regular means
of transport on the Albany River in 1779.

The general use of canoes in the Canadian fur trade
came to an end two years after the union of the Hudson's
Bay and the North West companies. "In 1823 Sir
George Simpson found that canoe transport was too
expensive, and ordered that the York or Hudson Bay
boat . . . should be used over all the main trade routes
of the Hudson's Bay Company." [Edwin C. Guillet,
Pioneer Travel in Upper Canada, page 41.] Simpson
argued that the York boat was more efficient, carrying
greater amounts of goods and men at less cost. Perhaps
nearer to the truth was the fact that the Hudson's Bay

Company lacked skillful canoemen and canoe builders, and were often operating in areas of small or no birch trees. The majority of its working personnel in transportation were Orkney men from the Orkney Islands and accustomed only to boats.

"The inland boat's [York boat] great disadvantage became apparent on portages. Whereas one or two voyageurs could manhandle a canoe around a rapid, a whole crew was often not enough to move the inland boat overland, and had to be reinforced by other crews . . .

Before the boat could be moved at all, the boatmen had to cut a road ten feet through the bush, then lay rollers three feet apart along the trail. Poplar logs best served this purpose, especially if they were green and smooth-barked. Dew or rain made the bark slippery and the boats would then go over them as if on greased rollers." [J. W. Chalmers, *Fur Trade Governor: George Simpson, 1820–1860*, page 112.]

An original York boat, built in the early 20th century, is preserved at Lower Fort Garry, north of Winnipeg.

[York boat sketch adapted from photo taken by Ernest Oberholtzer, ca. 1910. Courtesy, Oberholtzer Foundation.]

THE PORTAGE POLE CART

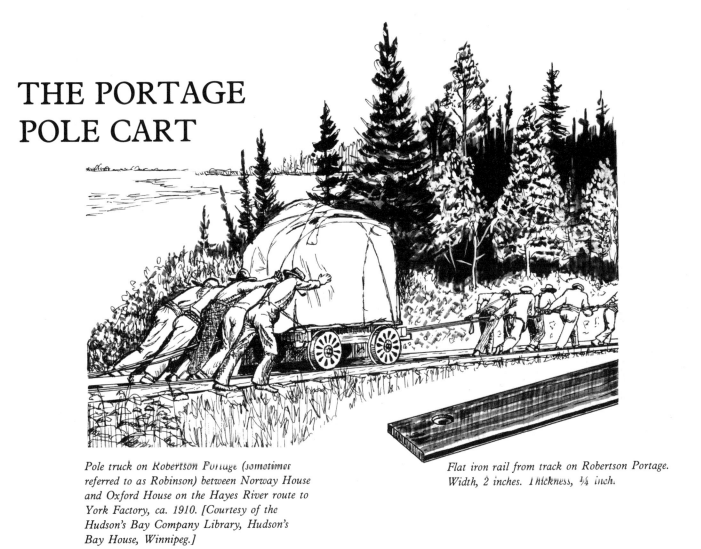

Pole truck on Robertson Portage (sometimes referred to as Robinson) between Norway House and Oxford House on the Hayes River route to York Factory, ca. 1910. [Courtesy of the Hudson's Bay Company Library, Hudson's Bay House, Winnipeg.]

Flat iron rail from track on Robertson Portage. Width, 2 inches. Thickness, ¼ inch.

When the large cargo-carrying York boats were put into use by the Hudson's Bay Company, the method of portaging craft changed drastically. Unlike the bark canoes, which were carried on the backs of the voyageurs, the York boats were literally pulled, pushed and rolled across the portages by sweating men. "On my return I found the canoes had arrived, and the people were busy carrying the baggage over the portage. This is upward of a mile long, but would be a very good road, were it not that the H. B. Co., from York Factory, with large boats, are in the habit of laying down a succession of logs from one end to the other for the purpose of rolling their boats over." [*The Manuscript Journals of Alexander Henry and David Thompson, 1799–1814*, Vol. II, page 463.]

In the late nineteenth century, the problems of transportation along the old water routes increased, and ways were sought to solve them. These problems were often at the portages. In some cases Red River carts were employed to transport cargo, and in at least two others rail systems were devised. On the one-mile Robertson Portage, a crude rail-cart arrangement was put into operation. Straps of iron were fastened to parallel logs to form rails over which men pulled wooden carts with iron wheels. York boats and tons of goods and supplies were moved across the portage in this fashion. As awkward as this may seem it was a great improvement over carrying the supplies on men's backs. A much more elaborate rail system, at a cost of $16,500, was installed in 1877 on the three-and-a-half mile portage around the Grand Rapids of the Saskatchewan. A firm in St. Paul, Minnesota, provided the four-wheel cars for $137 each. Actual rails were used, and horses were employed to pull the cars. On these, passengers as well as cargo were transported. Like the canoes of the French voyageurs, the York boats, except on the more remote routes, became casualties, replaced by steamboats, which themselves were eventually replaced by the advancing railroads. In the early twentieth century, with the development of the outboard motor, the canoe paddles no longer flashed in the sunlight.

As late as 1969, an old Chipewyan woman at Patuanak, near Ile à la Crosse, told the author she remembered in her youth seeing the men working on the York boats along the Churchill River.

RED RIVER CARTS

The earliest carts had solid wheels sawn from large logs.

Original Red River cart is in the collections of the Minnesota Historical Society. Length, 11 feet, 2 inches. Width (hub to hub), 5 feet, 7 inches. Wheel diameter, 5 feet, 3½ inches.

The Red River cart probably originated in Europe, as similar conveyances have been used in recent times in Spain, Russia, and the Balkans. The French traders, according to Eric Ross in *Beyond the River and the Bay*, pages 73–74, had carts in the Northwest. "These had been used in the Red River area where the ground is so smooth and level that they could travel in any direction. More recently the North West Company has re-introduced carts into the same area. The first of these seem to have been built at Pembina River House in 1801."

An important use of the cart was the transportation of buffalo robes and tongues, pemmican, and furs to St. Paul from the Pembina region. The cart was in general use as a commercial vehicle from the early 1840's to the late 1860's. The Red River cart was also extensively used on the Canadian prairies. According to Alexander Henry the Younger in 1803, "This invention [the cart] is worth four horses to us, as it would require five horses to carry as much on their backs as one will drag in each of those large carts." [*The Manuscript Journals of Alex-*

ander Henry and David Thompson, 1799–1814, Vol. 1, page 211.]

One of the most colorful descriptions of the Red River cart is given by Col. Hankins in his book *Dakota Land; or The Beauty of St. Paul*, pages 66–67: "The most singular feature of the cart and harness is that not a particle of iron need be used in their construction. Only ash or swamp-oak wood, roughly hewn with hatchets, forms the vehicle. . . . Nine hundred pounds is considered a good load for an Ox-cart, and thirty miles far enough to travel in one day. . . . An army of one hundred thousand crazy soldiers, marching with a *calithumpian* band, could not surpass the awful noise made by a train of several hundred Ox-cart wheels when in motion. The axle-trees are greased with a composition of lye and buffalo fat, which quickly slushes out, leaving the friction to produce the most doleful sounds ever devised to torture human ears or to demoralize a sensitive mind. A lazy, creaking whine, as if all the imps of pandemonium were singing themselves to sleep after a high old spree."

The Trading Place

"We crossed Beaver Lake on the first day of November [1775]; and the very next morning it was frozen over. Happily we were now at a place abounding with fish; and here, therefore, we resolved on wintering . . . our forty men were divided into three parties. . . . The third party was employed in building our house, our fort; and, in this within ten days, we saw ourselves commodiously lodged." [Alexander Henry, *Travels and Adventures in Canada and the Indian Territories Between the Years 1760 and 1776*, page 264.]

THE TRADING HOUSE
ON THE YELLOW RIVER

Main Building

To date unexcavated

Artist's conception of North West Company post on the Yellow River in northwestern Wisconsin, 1802–1803, based on archaeologist Edgar Oerichbauer's excavations.

"*We did not make palaces . . .* " So wrote George Nelson, a clerk for the XY Company in the St. Croix Valley during the years 1802–1803. In 1802, at the age of sixteen, he became an apprentice clerk for the offshoot rival of the North West Company. Nelson and his companions, following the customary route west from Montreal to Lake Superior, ascended the Brule and portaged into the St. Croix. On the Yellow River, a tributary of the St. Croix, they built some sixty yards from the North West post illustrated here. At this site the two competing companies carried on a winter's trading with the native Ojibwa. [*A Winter in the St. Croix Valley: George Nelson's Reminiscences, 1802–1803*, pages 24–25.]

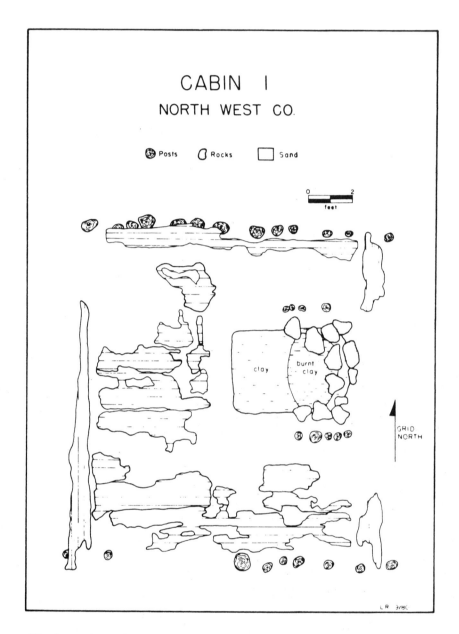

CABIN I
NORTH WEST CO.

Posts   Rocks   Sand

0   2
feet

clay   burnt
        clay

GRID
NORTH

L R 3/80

Archaeological evidence of stockade wall.

CABIN I

F 21

The sketch of the 1802–3 Yellow River post showing the complete cabin was based on evidence revealed by archaeologist Edgar Oerichbauer's excavation. Post molds left from vertical timbers, floor planking, door opening, fireplace, and collapsed walls reveal the size and nature of the primitive architecture.

Such wintering posts were often crudely constructed and occupied for only a single season. "From the simplicity of the construction ["*pieux en terre*" or stakes in the ground] & the season of the year, we always haste to put ourselves under Shelter. The N. W. Co. also soon finished theirs which they surrounded with stockades, about ten feet out of the ground, with two Bastions, loop holes &c in case of an attack from the Sioux, whose visit we had more than ordinary reasons to apprehend." [*A Winter in the St. Croix Valley: George Nelson's Reminiscences, 1802–1803*, pages 24–25.]

THE SANDY LAKE POST

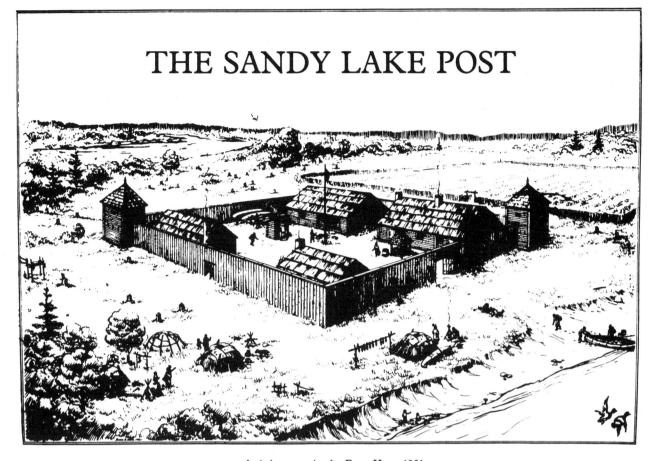

Artist's conception by Evan Hart, 1961.

In 1794 the North West Company, well within American territory, built a substantial post on a point extending from the west side of Sandy Lake. It was strategically situated on the important trade route between Fond du Lac, on the western end of Lake Superior, and the Mississippi River and constituted the western end of the well-known Savanna Portage. Like so many other posts built during the eighteenth and early nineteenth centuries in territory occupied by the British, the architecture was *"pieces sur pieces"* or log-on-log with the upright or vertical timbers in the ground. Later, when more permanent structures were needed, the uprights were placed on sill logs and called post-on-sill or Red River frame. This architecture had its origin in New France.

In January, 1806, Lieutenant Zebulon Pike, under orders from the U. S. War Department, led an expedition up the Mississippi River and visited the Sandy Lake post. On arrival, they were surprised to find a large stockade. "The establishment of this place was formed 12 years since by the N. W. Company . . . " [*The Expeditions of Zebulon Montgomery Pike*, Vol. I, page 139.]

It is evident from archaeological excavations carried out at the sites of two North West Company wintering posts and with historical documentation, that they were built with haste. The Yellow River post in Northwestern Wisconsin and the John Sayer post on the Snake River in east-central Minnesota were occupied for only a year or two. As an example of the speed in building these posts, Sayer on the Snake put his men to work on October 9, 1804, clearing a spot on which to build. On November 21 his men were erecting a flag pole. Buildings with roofs, floors, and chimneys and a surrounding stockade were completed, and he was ready for business. George Nelson, the clerk at the Yellow River XY post, describes the construction of his establishment in 1802: "We built up the two sides, to the height required, say five and a half, or perhaps six feet. These are secured by two stakes at each end, as a common rail fence, & braced by a good strong stick, the whole breadth of the house & notched at each end, to lay on the two sides, to prevent their moving." Nelson goes on to describe how the houses are plastered, the chimneys made, and the roof covered with sod as a preservative against fire. Young George Nelson adds: "Tho' thus roughly & rudely constructed, we soon get accustomed, & when we have enough to eat we feel comfortable; for, here as everywhere else, we live in anticipation of better times & never, at least very few of us know to enjoy what we possess." [*A Winter in the St. Croix Valley: George Nelson's Reminiscences, 1802-03*, pages 24–25.]

Another trader, in a different location, writes: "We fixed close to the lake side, where we erected a loghouse, thirty feet long, and twenty feet wide, divided into two apartments, into which we deposited our goods. The next concern was to conceal our canoes in the woods, and to hide the rum underground, except a small quantity for immediate use, knowing by experience the necessity of keeping it from the Indians, as our safety so essentially depended on it." [J. Long, *Voyages and Travels of an Indian Interpreter and Trader, 1791*, page 54.]

In the sixteenth and early seventeenth centuries, when the fur trade was active along the St. Lawrence River, the Indians brought their furs to the traders. However, once the traders moved into the distant areas to the northwest, they found it necessary to spend the winters in the Indian country. The earliest traders, the French *couriers des bois*, probably lived much as the Indians in meager dwellings, mere huts. Later, as the interior trading operations increased in size and personnel, so did the posts. The trading or wintering posts were always built in a location convenient to the local Indians, on either a navigable river or a lake accessible by river.

HIGH WINE

Spigot. Length, 6 inches

Spigot collars.
Diameter, 7/8 inch

Spigot key.
Length, 2½ inches

Kegs and barrels were not only used for liquors but for other commodities as well, including flour, salt, sugar, gunpowder, pork, and beef in brine.

One of the most common uses for the keg was for high wine, and a popular size was the nine-gallon keg. "Every trader knows that most of the quarrels between the natives and the whites, and among the natives themselves,

are precipitated by alcohol; but he also knows that as long as competition continues to persist he, and all his fellow traders, will be powerless to stop the traffic, even should he be of a mind to do so, for in some areas the Indians will not trade furs for anything else . . . cheap rum from the West Indies can be sent into the northwest in a concentrated form which can then be easily diluted and sold where the demand is great. The more accustomed a tribe has become to drink, the stronger is the mixture sold to them. For the Blackfeet, who have been trading a relatively short time, a nine-gallon keg contains only four or five quarts of high wine mixed with water. But for the western Crees and Assiniboines six quarts of high wine are added, and for the hard drinking Ojibwas, eight or even nine quarts." [Eric Ross, *Beyond the River and the Bay*, page 51.]

"Mr. Shaw being a dashing Bourgeois gave the men of my fifteen canoes a dram out of a big keg he had upon Tap." ["The Diary of John Macdonell," *Five Fur Traders of the Northwest*, pages 100–101.]

The spigot and cylindrical brass collars were excavated at Grand Portage. A spigot assembly consisted of the brass spigot, a cylindrical collar, and a key with a design which fitted into the collar. The key illustrated was found by Bob Taraldson on Saganaga Lake, a link in the chain of lakes and rivers forming the Grand Portage route. [Spigot and cylindrical collars from Alan R. Woolworth, "Grand Portage Archaeological Report, 1975."]

GIFT GIVING

John Jacob Astor Medal

The practice of presenting medals to the Indians by the fur companies was late compared to the gift-giving to stimulate trade. The gifts first given, usually to the chiefs or leaders, were such items as awls, beads, guns, powder, shot and liquor. In the later period of the trade, chiefs' coats were also given.

The Astor medal, two-and-a-half inches in diameter, belonged to Gabriel Franchère, one of the party founding Astoria on the Oregon coast for the American Fur Company. Dr. Frederick Franchère, great-great grandson of Gabriel Franchère, presented the rare medal to the Minneota Historical Society in 1966. Silver medals, designed for presentation to Indian chiefs and warriors, were given by both governments and fur-trading companies. Medals were given to Indian chiefs on important occasions, such as the signing of a treaty, and they played an important part in establishing peace and

friendship with the Indians. Before the War of 1812, the British presented many medals bearing the image of King George III. The American Fur Company attempted to get the United States government to furnish presents to distribute to the Indians, but, that failing, the Company proceeded to have Indian medals made on its own. The silver Astor medals were close imitations of the official American peace medals. All such medals, official and otherwise, were prized by the Indians. Flags were also presented, but perhaps were less valued.

The Indians often initiated the gift giving: "The great chief, whose name was Kesconeek, made me a present of skins, dried meat, fish, and wild oats [rice]; a civility which I returned without delay, and in a manner with which he seemed highly gratified." [J. Long, *Voyages and Travels of an Indian Interpreter and Trader, 1791*, page 55.]

A CANOE LOAD OF MERCHANDISE

May 25, 1725, invoice for merchandise from the business records of a Montreal merchant.

INVOICE for merchandise sold and shipped to Messrs. Clignancour and Mogras at "La Bée" [i.e., "La Baie" for Green Bay, Wisconsin], on their account and at their own risk, following instructions and memorandum received:

No 1		*One bale containing:*			
	2	pieces of woolen cloth worth 114 pounds [weight] of dry beaver apiece, payable in kind, both pieces totalling 228 pounds of beaver at 38s		433£4s	
	18	pairs of sleeves, of woolen cloth,	at 5£	90"	
	12	ditto, of red Molton	at 5£	60"	624" 9" 0"
	2	2-pt blankets	at 14£	28"	
	8	quires of paper	at 20s	8"	
	1½	ell strong *Mélis* canvas	at 3£10s	5" 5"	

No 2		*One bale containing:*			
	2	pieces of woolen cloth worth 114 pounds [of beaver], both pieces totalling 228 pounds at 38s		433" 4"	
	18	pairs of sleeves, of Molton cloth,	at 5£	40"	
	22	pairs of sleeves, of woolen cloth,	at 5£	110"	676" 9" 0"
	12	men's shirts, large size	at 5£	60"	
	2	2-pt blankets	at 14£	28"	
	1½	ell strong *Mélis* canvas	at 3£10s	5" 5"	

No 3		*One bale containing:*			
	2	pieces of blue woolen cloth worth 228 pounds of dry beaver, at 38s		433" 4"	
	18	women's shirts	at 4£	72"	
	12	ditto	at 40s	24"	
	12	"Tapabort" [*Tapabord*: old type of deerstalker cap]	at 3£10s	42"	668"19" 0"
	3	small *capots*	at 5£10s	16"10"	
	4	ditto, larger size	at 7£10s	30"	
	2	2-pt blankets	at 14£	28"	
	1½	ell strong *Mélis* canvas		5" 5"	

					1969"17" 0"

[Marie Gérin-Lajoie and Kenneth Kidd, "Montreal Merchants' Records, 1708–1775," mimeographed. Translation by Marie Gérin-Lajoie.]

The foregoing is a page from the business records of six Montreal merchants (1708-1775) who furnished fur traders with goods and supplies. The original records were discovered and translated by the Minnesota Historical Society's historical researcher, Marie Gérin-Lajoie. An unpublished manuscript dealing with these records, by Marie Gérin-Lajoie and Kenneth Kidd, is in the manuscript division of the Minnesota Historical Society in St. Paul. The records consist largely of hundreds of inventories of canoe loads of merchandise shipped to posts in the area of the Great Lakes, the Northwest, and the Mississippi River country, plus business transactions with local suppliers. Marie Gérin-Lajoie has provided a translation from the now-archaic French.

Once the fur trade had developed to the point where traders operating in the interior required supplies of goods and equipment in quantity, business men or merchants in Montreal served this function. Acting as importers of goods from Europe and from the cottage industries of New France, they filled the orders of not only the goods traded, but also canoes, equipment, and provisions. It was the merchants who made up the inventories of each canoe load heading west, charged to a certain trader for a specific location. Careful records were kept.

"The merchant in Montreal not only secured the goods from England [or France], purchased the canoes and hired the men, but also directed the route of the canoes and arranged for provisions and supplies necessary for the journey . . . Cooperation was essential between the London [or French] house, the Montreal merchant, and the trader in the interior . . . " [Harold A. Innis, *The Fur Trade in Canada*, pages 211–212.]

CANOE NUMBER 17 IN THE BRIGADE

Bill of Lading of Canoe No. 17

N. W. MARK.			Men's Names.
	4	Bales Goods,	1 *Fra. Crustois Fp.*
		" Twift,	2 *J. ... ... S.*
	1	Carrot,	3 *Jn. Harnois M.*
	1	" Kettles,	4 *La. Ambault "*
	1	Kegs Powder,	5 *Andre Harnois "*
	3	" Spirits,	6 *Jn. Bouché — "*
		· High Wines,	
		White Sugar,	
		Brown,	Provifions.
		Pork,	
		Beef,	½ Keg Greafe,
	1	" Butter,	1⅓ Bufhels Corn,
		Shrub,	⅓ " Oats
		Madeira,	
		Port,	
		Salt,	Agrès complete.
		Bag Flour,	
	2	Cafes Iron No.	1 *Kettle*
		Hats,	1 *Oil Cloth*
		Knives,	1 *Spunge*
	1	" Guns,	1 *Line*
		Soap,	1 *Ax*
		Traps,	1 *Sail*
		Caffette No.	5 tts *Gum*
		Maccaron,	1 *Bunch Wattap*
	2	Bags fhot,	1 *fm. Bark*
	2	" Balls.	
	19	Pieces,	

Bill of Lading, dated 1806, of a North West Company canoe loaded at Fort William. [Courtesy, McCord Museum, McGill University, Montreal.]

This 1806 bill of lading of canoe number 17 tells an interesting story. There were at least seventeen canoes in the brigade leaving Fort William. The nineteen pieces or bales was the average load of a North canoe traveling over the Kaministiquia route. Note the names of the six French Canadian voyageurs and their respective positions or assignments in the canoe. Number 1, the foreman or bowman; number 2, the steerman; and 3, 4, 5, and 6, the midmen. Note also the provisions carried, the grease, the corn and the oats [wild rice]. In the 1960's at Berens River, Manitoba, the author, pointing to some wild rice growing along the shore, asked a local Indian what it was, knowing full well what it was. The answer was "oats," a term carried over from the days of the fur trade. Lastly, notice the equipment carried for use enroute, including patching material—bark, gum, and watap—for the canoe in case of mishap. [Original bill of lading in the McCord Museum, McGill University, Montreal.]

THE FUR PRESS AND FUR PACKS

Since goods and furs were transported in canoes and boats and on the backs of men, "pieces" or bales had to be made up in manageable amounts. The standard-size piece was established early at ninety pounds. Two of these became the acceptable load for one man to carry over a portage, and one piece, a convenient size to lift into and out of a canoe or boat.

Engagés (voyageurs) organized the pelts in pieces. The loose furs were placed in the press and weight was applied on the long pole by several voyageurs. Ropes seen running from the bottom of the press were used to tie and secure each piece.

"Tuesday [May] 26 [1801] Yesterday our people finished making our furs into packs, of ninety pounds weight each. Two or three of these made a load for a man, to carry across the portages." [Daniel Williams Harmon, *A Journal of Voyages and Travels in the Interior of North America*, page 50.]

"Mr. McKinzie's two outfits or equipments had arrived from their trading posts. They called to see me, and I was informed by them that the furs they had brought on here, were to be packed in a certain way, for transportation by canoe to Montreal. At it I went, and before Mr. McKinzie arrived in a light canoe, the forty or fifty packs were pressed, marked, and the bills of the contents of each pack all ready." [*Wisconsin Historical Collections*, Vol. 9, page 143.]

Packs or bales of raw beaver pelts, adapted from an early photograph of Colin Fraser shown with furs he had bought from trappers in the Northwest Territories.

KEEPING THE RECORDS STRAIGHT

Figure 1. Candle holder

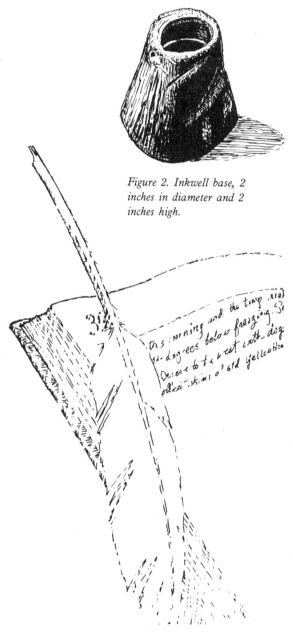

Figure 2. Inkwell base, 2 inches in diameter and 2 inches high.

The principal duty of a clerk in the fur trade was the keeping of records, both at the wintering post and at the depot and rendezvous. Indian credits had to be recorded, furs counted, and goods packed and marked for transport. Traders themselves often kept diaries and journals which recorded daily events and observations at the posts. Hudson's Bay traders were required by regulation to observe and record the "goings on" of their competitors, today a valuable source of information about French, independent, and North West Company traders whose records for the most part have been lost or destroyed.

Copper candlestick base (incomplete) was found in the mud shallows near the North West Company's Fort Charlotte dock structure, Grand Portage. [Minnesota Historical Society collections.] It was probably used by a clerk or *bourgeois* of the North West Company at Fort Charlotte, the western terminus of the Grand Portage, during the period 1785–1802. Only the base remains, with the rest of the candle holder reconstructed by the artist.

The lead inkwell was found on the site of John Sayer's North West Company post on the Snake River near Pine City, Minnesota. The inkwell may have been used by Sayer to write his diary of 1804–1805. [Joseph A. Neubauer collection.]

"Sunday 7th. [November, 1804] Fine Weather. Com-

pleated all the Indian Credits & gave them 2 large Kegs being in 2 separate Bands to encourage them to Hunt well. went with 2 Men in a Canoe in search of a More Convenient place to Build. found a more eligible Spot about a Mile up the River." [*Five Fur Traders of the Northwest*, page 253.] Research by historical archaeologist, Douglas Birk, has revealed that John Sayer, North West Company trader, was the author of the so-called "Thomas Connor Diary."

The Gathering

"Unlike other frontiers, the fur trade had little place

for dead Indians. Almost universally the native was an

integral part of the fur trade operation. He brought in the

bulk of the pelts and robes . . . " [Lewis O. Saum,

The Fur Trader and the Indian, page 42.]

THE FURS

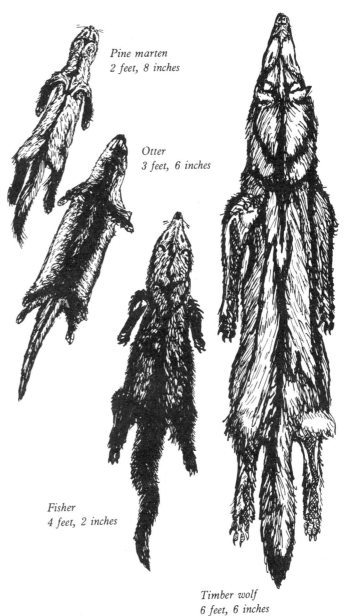

Beaver
2 feet, 9 inches
by 2 feet, 4 inches

Pine marten
2 feet, 8 inches

Otter
3 feet, 6 inches

Fisher
4 feet, 2 inches

Timber wolf
6 feet, 6 inches

Until the European wanted furs, animals to the Indians meant only food and clothing. They took only what they needed. Once the trade in furs had begun in earnest, the traders were quick to realize that furs taken in winter, especially in the northern latitudes, were far superior to those taken in summer or in areas to the south. Even in the winter months, there were times when the fur was superior or "prime," and this varied with the animals. Ordinarily, those taken from November to February were considered the best. In those winter months, the animal needed the maximum protection from the cold, hence the better fur.

The most profitable fur was that of the marten. "In 1545 Jean Alphonse tells us that the Indians of Norumbega on the New England coast possessed large quantities of furs, and he mentions especially marten, a fur then so rare in Europe that only princes and great lords could wear it." [H. P. Biggar, *The Early Trading Companies of New France*, page 31.]

The most sought-after fur was that of the beaver. "The abundance of beaver in the forest belt of the north, the extraordinary ease of transportation in birch-bark canoes by these numerous water-ways, the great value of the beaver wool in the eyes of the fashionable hat-makers of Europe—these were factors in the development of the fur trade and went to making the history of the Northwest." [Arthur S. Morton, *A History of the Canadian West to 1870–1871*, page 24.]

The most valuable fur was that of the black fox. Other animals taken for their furs were mink, muskrats, red fox, lynx, deer, bear, buffalo and wolverine.

"We likewise made signs to them [the Indians] that we wished them no harm, and sent two men on shore to offer them some knives and other iron goods, and a red cap to give to their chief . . . . They bartered all [the furs] they had to such an extent that all went back naked without anything on them; and they made signs to us that they would return on the morrow with more furs." [Cameron Nish, tr., *The French Regime*, page 5.]

SNARES

Snare for lynx and fox

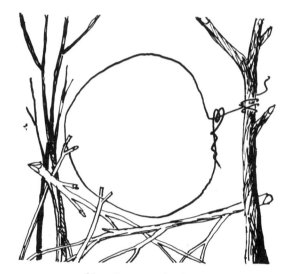

Shore-line snare for fox

The native Americans, before any contact with the European's guns and steel traps, used a number of methods to kill and catch animals. Among these were snares, deadfalls, spears, harpoons, arrows, and driving large animals, like buffalo, over cliffs or into pounds. Of these, snaring was one of the most common methods. The loop of snare wire was suspended from a fallen tree in such a way that the animal walking through it would be caught. Its struggles would tighten the snare, and death by strangulation would most often result. Snares were fastened to an immovable object like a tree or to a movable object such as a log. Snares were most effective on animals which used trails. Before contact with Europeans, the native Americans used loops of *babiche* (raw hide).

"These huntsmen, as soon as they have erected their huts, employ themselves in making snares for otters, foxes, bears, land-beavers, and martens, on the borders of lakes; which when placed, they regularly visit every day." [George Heriot, *Travels Through the Canadas*, Vol. II, page 501.]

The spring pole snare was commonly used for rabbits, an important source of food. "The Indians live here [Fort Frances] as at Rat Portage [Kenora], on rice, fish, and rabbits. The last are so numerous in the winter, that one man caught eighty-six in one night, being only unsuccessful with fourteen snares out of the hundred he had set in the evening." [Paul Kane, *Wanderings of an Artist*, page 320.]

Spring-pole snare

DEADFALLS AND TRAPS

Another common type of trap was the deadfall in which an animal, trying to take the bait, disturbed the trigger, causing a heavy log to fall on its back, killing it. The deadfall was most effective on animals which were tempted by bait, like fish or raw meat. Those caught by this type of trap were martens, fisher, mink, otter, and ermine.

"Not far from Charron Lake I made a camp one time. I built up lots of deadfalls, Indian trap. I had eighteen fishers that time which made up a lot of fur. Easy to kill a fisher in deadfalls." [Tom Boulanger, *An Indian Remembers: My Life as a Trapper in Northern Manitoba*, page 46.]

The steel trap, a late introduction, was mentioned by David Thompson in the 1790's. Indians were slow to use the steel trap, considering it too heavy to carry into the wilderness from camp to camp. First the product of blacksmiths, it was Sewell Newhouse who began the steel-trap industry when he turned out his handmade traps from scythes, axe heads, and files, in 1823.

Deadfall

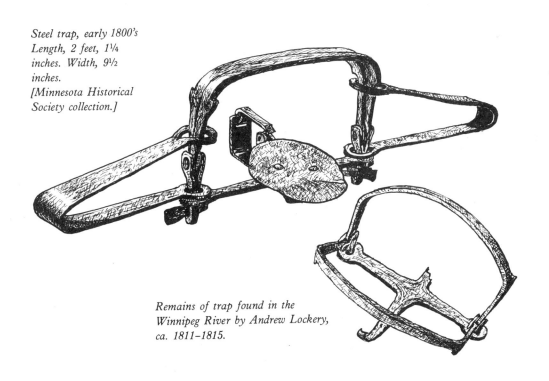

Steel trap, early 1800's Length, 2 feet, 1¼ inches. Width, 9½ inches. [Minnesota Historical Society collection.]

Remains of trap found in the Winnipeg River by Andrew Lockery, ca. 1811–1815.

53

Figure 1

Figure 2

Figure 3

THE SUGAR BUSH

Alexander Mackenzie tells of a small village, composed of a few Algonquin families and several whites, at the eastern end of Lake Superior. With a shortage of game, the villagers lived on a diet of white fish and potatoes, and added to this, maple sugar. "In the spring of the year they, and other inhabitants, make a quantity of sugar from the maple tree, which they exchange with the traders for necessary articles, or carry it to Michilimackinac where they expect a better price." [*The Journals and Letters of Sir Alexander Mackenzie*, page 93.]

An important source of food for the Indian was the maple tree. In the spring of the year, when the sap was beginning to run, it was collected and boiled down for syrup and sugar. At times, in areas of no maple trees, birch trees were tapped.

"Each family or group of two or three families had its own sugar bush . . . and the people went there in the early spring to make the year's supply of sugar. Two structures remained in the sugar camp from year to year. These were the birch-bark lodge in which the utensils were stored, and the frame of the lodge in which the sugar was made . . . . Among the articles that were not stored but carried each year to the camps were the large brass kettles for boiling sap." [Frances Densmore, *Uses of Plants by the Chippewa Indians, 1926–27*, pages 308–313.]

In 1983 Frank Dolence, of rural Hibbing, Minnesota,

Figure 4

Makuks holding sixty
pounds of maple sugar

[Illustrations are based on a watercolor by Seth Eastman.]

donated maple sugar-making items, which he had found years earlier in northeastern Minnesota, to the Minnesota Historical Society. On a high ridge in a grove of aged maples, he came upon the collapsed remains of a birch-bark lodge under which were found numerous bark and wooden utensils used for making sugar. Among them were ladles (Fig. 1), makuks (Fig. 2), baskets to catch sap (Fig. 4), and wooden "spiles" or sharpened pieces of cedar (Fig. 3) which were driven into the tree and along which the sap dripped. "This tree [the sugar maple] grows abundantly on the St. Croix, and affords to the Chippewas an important article of diet. Some Indian families manufacture 1000 pounds annually. We frequently saw their sap troughs by the roadside, and

could not but admire the ingenuity and simplicity of their construction. A rectangular piece of birchbark, about eighteen by twenty inches, is plaited with two folds at each end, which are secured in their places by a string made of the bark of the linden-tree; thus forming a tight and elastic square vessel, capable of holding a gallon or more." [E.S. Seymour, *Sketches of Minnesota: The New England of the West . . . 1849*, page 195.] Most of the items found by Dolence were in poor condition. At some distance away from the long-abandoned camp, under a pile of brush, he found a large and remarkably well preserved brass kettle. No doubt the Indian woman decided to hide it rather than carry the heavy kettle back to camp.

The Trade Goods

"European goods were in greater demand among the Indians as old cultural traits disappeared . . . Peter Kalm at the end of the period [mid seventeen hundreds] noted the ever-prevalent manner in which European goods had become a part of Indian economy." [Harold A. Innis, *The Fur Trade in Canada*, page 109.]

KETTLES

Of the many trade items offered by the Europeans, few had greater impact on the Indian than the kettle, gun, and the hatchet. Kettles were often manufactured in "nests" for the purpose of transporting, thus taking up less space in the ship and canoe. On arrival at the trading site, they were sold separately. The iron bail [handle] was not attached in shipment, but was fastened to the kettle later.

"An unbreakable, unburnable iron or brass kettle wiped out at a stroke all the labour and care incidental to a whole series of wooden, bark or even pottery vessels." [John Bartlet Brebner, *The Explorers of North America*, page 105.]

"Above everything the kettle has always seemed to them, and seems still, the most valuable article they can obtain from us." [Nicolas Denys, *Description and Natural History of the Coasts of North America, 1672*, in Harold A. Innis, *The Fur Trade in Canada*, page 18.]

Lidded copper kettle, 4½ inches in diameter and 4 5/8 inches high, of a type traded by the Hudson's Bay Company from the 1780's until the early 20th century and available in a variety of sizes. This one-quart specimen is from the Lac La Croix Indian Reservation.

Probably the maker's mark

Copper kettle with dog-eared lugs and "hammered" bowl— approximately 11 inches in diameter. Note patch on kettle base. [Adapted from W. A. Kenyon: The Grimsby Site, *Royal Ontario Museum.] Excavated from Neutral Indians burial grounds, used in the early seventeenth century. According to W. A. Kenyon, curator of archaeology, Royal Ontario Museum, the first European to visit the Neutrals may have been the young Frenchman, Etienne Brulé.*

17 brass nested kettles (sizes, 6 inches to 20 inches in diameter) found in 1960 in Horsetail Rapids on the Granite River. A find of three nested sets in the early eighteenth-century Tunica burial grounds is similar. [Jeffrey B. Brain, Tunica Treasure, *page 168.]*

KNIVES

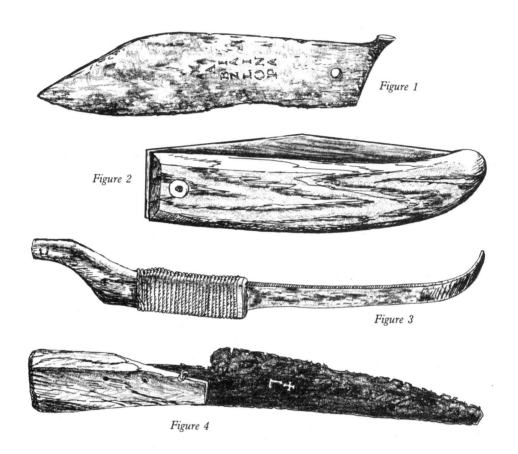

Figure 1

Figure 2

Figure 3

Figure 4

Knives had a special importance to the Indian, and, in fact, to anyone living on the frontier where a handy cutting tool was needed. Some were worn in sheaths on the belt for immediate use. Other knives available from the traders were clasp or pocket knives and those for butchering and carving. Perhaps the greatest utility for the knife was for skinning and cutting meat.

Figure 1 The knife blade illustrated was found at Fort St. Charles, the post established by Pierre La Vérendrye on Lake of the Woods in 1732. It is of the type used in the folding or clasp knife shown in Figure 2.

Figure 2 One of sixteen French-eared knives of a folding variety found in the Winnipeg River. Length, 5¼ inches.

Figure 3 Crooked knife collected from Grand Portage in 1930. The blade, made from an iron or steel file, was inserted into a wooden handle and held by a tightly-wrapped cord. According to the 1688 inventory of an independent trader, crooked knives were already reaching the Illinois country. Listed among numerous trade items were "6 dozen canoe [crooked] knives." [Mary

Elizabeth Good, *Guebert Site: An 18th century historic KASKASKIA INDIAN VILLAGE*, page 8.]

"Beyond the circumpolar region its [the crooked knife's] usefulness is limited by the presence or absence of the birch tree, for it was used mostly in making birch-bark canoes. Ribs, gunwales and other wooden elements were best fashioned by means of a crooked knife." [Marie Gérin-Lajoie and Kenneth Kidd, "Montreal Merchants' Records," mimeographed.] "The men hunt, build canoes, (which the women sew and pitch,) snow-shoe frames ready to net and which the women must finish; they make axe helves, paddles, *traines* for hauling in winter and every other crooked knife work." [L. R. Masson, *Les Bourgeois de la Compagnie du Nord-Ouest*, page 257.]

Figure 4 The cross-and-L knife has been found at fur-trading sites throughout the Northwest. Length of entire specimen, 9½ inches.

[Artifacts, Figures 1, 3 and 4 from the collections of the Minnesota Historical Society. Artifact, Figure 2, from the Royal Ontario Museum.]

AXES AND TOMAHAWKS

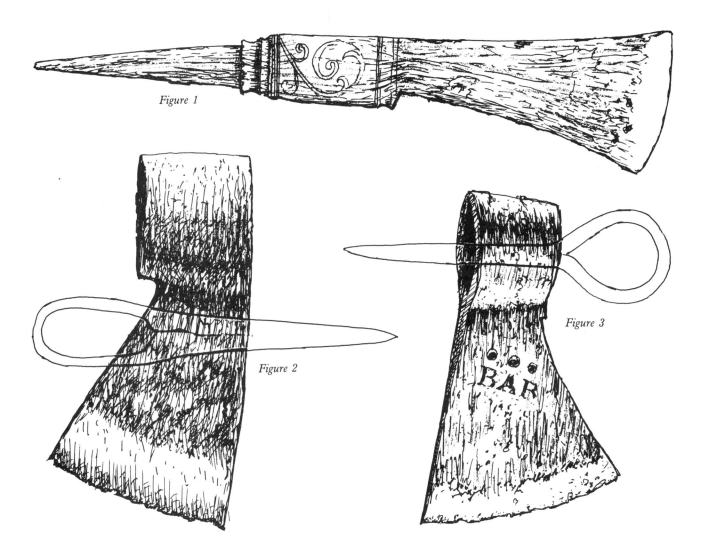

Figure 1

Figure 2

Figure 3

The iron axe, one of the earliest items offered in trade, was an immediate attraction to the Indian. Huge axes of the "felling" type have been found in sixteenth and early seventeenth-century graves in eastern Canada. Trade axes were imported in great numbers and a variety of sizes. These were shipped to the wintering posts in wooden crates. Handles were fashioned and installed by the buyers.

"Axes and hatchets were ordinarily imported in New France, and most of these must have come from France itself, though the makers and exact locations are usually unknown. Both the Montreal merchants and the Hudson's Bay Company imported both axes and hatchets labelled 'Biscay' or 'Biscayne,' usually the latter, and it has generally been assumed, without concrete evidence to this effect, that these came from the Biscay Region of

France." [Marie Gérin-Lajoie and Kenneth Kidd, "Montreal Merchants' Records," mimeographed.] The merchants' records also mentioned several kinds of tomahawks, including spiked tomahawks.

Figure 1 Spiked tomahawk recovered from the Winnipeg River by the Quetico-Superior Project divers in 1966. Length, 10¾ inches. Note the fine craftsmanship and inlay design still evident on the speciman. [Royal Ontario Museum collection.]

Figure 2 French iron axe, adapted from W. A. Kenyon, *The Grimsby Site*, Royal Ontario Museum. Approximate date, 1640's. Length, 8 inches.

Figure 3 One of 29 trade axes, labelled BAR, found in the Winnipeg River in 1966 with parts of the pine packing crate. Length, approximately 6¾ inches.

BLANKETS AND BEADS

Before the arrival of the European, the northern Indian relied heavily on animal furs and hides for clothing. The women were expert in tanning skins and could make them thick or thin, hard or soft as they wished. However, when European goods became available, woolen blankets soon replaced the fur and leather clothing. The Indian quickly saw the advantage of the lighter woolen cloth, for, even when wet, it provided more protection from the elements. "But we now plainly, as well as the Indians, see in this climate, the great advantage of woollen over leather clothing, the latter when wet sticks to the skin, and is very uncomfortable, requires time to dry, with caution to keep it to its shape of clothing. On the contrary the woollen, even when wet, is not uncomfortable . . . " [*David Thompson's Narrative of his Explorations in Western America, 1784–1812*, pages 421–422.]

Blankets were valued not only by the natives but by the traders and their employees as well. The woolen blankets were used for making capotes, coats, pants, gloves, bed covers, and as covering for the natives who often preferred blankets to coats.

When the Hudson's Bay Company introduced the point system in 1779, the Standard of Trade was a 1-point blanket for 1 prime beaver skin, a 2-point blanket for 2 beavers, and so on. With later inflation the blankets cost more in beaver skins. At some time after 1868, the Hudson's Bay Company standardized its blanket sizes with each point indicating a different weight and precise dimensions. Note the blanket illustration.

Although the Hudson's Bay and North West companies bought their blankets from several localities in England, it is safe to say that a large percentage of them came from the blanket makers of Witney. "The first mention of 'pointed' blankets in Hudson's Bay Company records is in the Minute Book of a meeting of the Committee on 16 December 1779. At that time a letter was written to Messrs. Empson of Witney (Oxfordshire) requesting samples of pointed blankets for inspection by the Committee. It appears that these blankets were already an article of trade, possibly in New England, Virginia, and New France . . . five hundred pair of 'pointed' blankets were immediately purchased." [Letter, March 30, 1983, to the author from Hudson's Bay Company Library, Winnipeg.]

The white or "common" blankets were popular with the Indians as they provided the best white camouflage. "Perhaps the most interesting items of trade goods were the blankets sent to York Fort. It had been reported that the Indians had preferred white cloth to red and blue

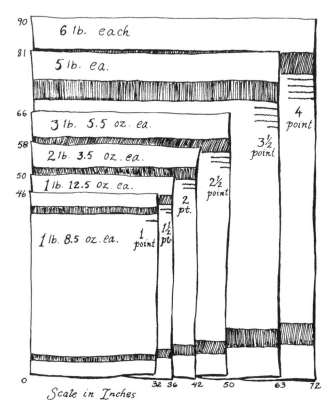

Blanket illustration adapted from Douglas Mackay, "Blanket Coverage," The Beaver, *June, 1935, page 45.*

which had hitherto been shipped, so a trial shipment of three white blankets was now sent; they were cheaper, and when worn they were not so likely to frighten the game in the snow-covered landscape." [E. E. Rich, *Hudson's Bay Company, 1670–1870*, Vol. I, page 254.]

BEADS

" . . . the bulk of the glass beads traded on the North American continent from the 16th until the first half of the 19th centuries were manufactured in the glass factories of Murano, Venice—since the 13th century the center of European glass production. . . . the glass trade bead—produced in one locality, has become the eyes of historians and students of the American Indian, the denominator of the fur trade." [Arthur Woodward, *Denominators of the Fur Trade: An Anthology of Writings on the Material Culture of the Fur Trade*, page 15.]

Two types of beads recovered from the Basswood River in 1961, by divers of the Quetico-Superior Research team. [Minnesota Historical Society collection.]

American Fur Company beads, ca. 1820–40. [Minnesota Historical Society collection.]

A glass bead from the early historic period, ca. 1610–1670. [Courtesy, Kenneth Kidd, Peterborough, Ontario.]

Beads, ca. 1732–1740, found on the surface at Fort St. Charles by Douglas Birk, Minnesota Historical Society archaeologist.

HARPOONS AND FILES

Figure 1

Of the two items of trade illustrated on this page, the file was by far the more important to the Indian. Iron axes, chisels, knives, and other edged tools had to be sharpened, and the file provided the only means. That the file was a significant item of trade is evidenced by its frequent appearance in quantity on the inventories of merchandise. In 1784, as in 1748, on the Hudson's Bay Company Standard of Trade, a large flat file traded for one beaver skin.

Figure 1 This harpoon of iron was found at Fort St. Charles on Lake of the Woods. Note how much this resembles the prehistoric bone harpoon. Established in 1732 by the French explorer-fur trader, Pierre Gaultier de Varennes, Sieur de La Vérendrye, the post served as

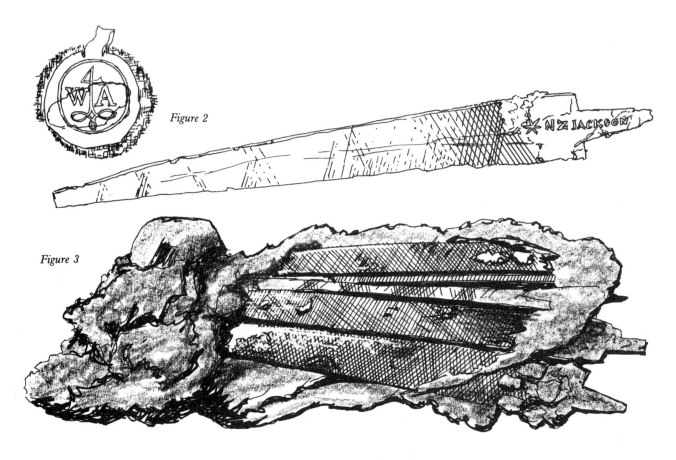

Figure 2

Figure 3

[Items illustrated from the collections of the Minnesota Historical Society.]

the jumping-off place for the posts he would build in the Lake Winnipeg country and on the Saskatchewan River.

Figure 2 A lead bale seal, marked W. A., was found in association with the bundle of files illustrated in figure 3. Note the remains of the cloth or duffle from the bag still held between the sides of the lead seal.

Figure 3 A bundle of thirty identical files was found at Horsetail Rapids on the Granite River in northern Min-

nesota by divers of the Quetico-Superior Project. Note the maker, "NZ Jackson." "As the Minnesota Historical Society has demonstrated, a collection of copper kettles or a cloth bag full of files recovered by divers can bring portage history to life in a way that no document can ever achieve." [Ivor Noël Hume, *A Guide to Artifacts of Colonial America*, page 7.]

FIRESTEELS, AWLS, THIMBLES, AND FISH HOOKS

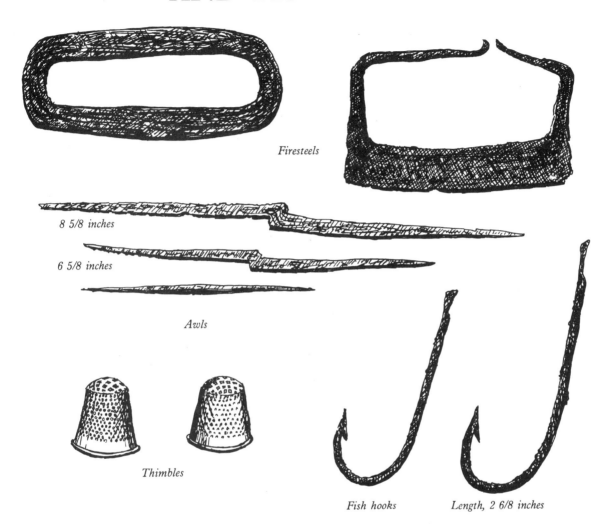

Firesteels

8 5/8 inches

6 5/8 inches

Awls

Thimbles

Fish hooks   *Length, 2 6/8 inches*

Firesteels, awls, thimbles, and fish hooks were all common and useful items found on the inventories of the traders. Firesteels were used to make fire when struck against flint. Awls were used to punch holes through bark and leather. Thimbles were used by the Indian women to protect fingers from sharp awls and needles when sewing. Fish hooks, of course, provided an effective means of securing an important food supply.

Montreal merchant Monière's first recorded sale of goods destined for the "Western Sea" on June 2–3, 1731, included "3 dozen strike-a-lites." This was an improvement over iron pyrites used formerly by the Indians to make fire.

The three awls shown above were excavated at Grand Portage. The canoe awl, the largest of these, was used to punch holes in the heavy birch bark for lashings of watap, the split root of the spruce tree. "I obtained for an awl, a passage to the next village, a distance of three miles through strong rapids." [*Simon Fraser Letters and Journals, 1806–1808*, page 86.]

The two brass thimbles illustrated measure 7/8 inches high by 3/4 inches in diameter. The thimbles were found by Quetico-Superior Project divers on the Basswood River west of Horse Portage in August, 1961. Eighteen similar thimbles were recovered from the Winnipeg River at Boundary Falls in 1966.

The flat-shanked fish hooks were excavated at the 1802–03 North West Company wintering post on the Yellow River in northwestern Wisconsin by archaeologist Edgar S. Oerichbauer.

[Firesteels, awls and thimbles from the collections of the Minnesota Historical Society.]

ICE CHISELS AND MUSKRAT SPEARS

Nineteen wrought-iron ice chisels (Figure 1) and six double-barbed iron spears (Figure 2) recovered from the Basswood River in July, 1961. [Minnesota Historical Society collections.]

Figure 1   Length, 18 inches

Figure 2   Length, 14¼ inches

Spearing muskrat

After the initial trading of knives, hatchets, kettles, and beads in the early years, the white man began to devise more effective methods for the Indians to increase the harvest of furs. Two items which were especially productive in the northern latitudes were ice chisels and spears.

"There is abundant evidence that great quantities of fur were obtained in America, by Indian and white hunter alike, during the seventeenth and eighteenth centuries without benefit of metal traps." [Carl P. Russell, *Firearms, Traps and Tools of the Mountain Men*, page 97.]

Spears, mounted on long wooden poles, of the type illustrated above, were a popular trade item and were used for spearing muskrats, beaver, and large fish. They closely resembled the prehistoric barbed spears fashioned from horn or bone.

Ice chisels, used to open frozen beaver lodges, were popular with inland tribes. The ice chisel and a strong net made of sinew or cordage figured importantly in the winter beaver hunt, which required the cooperation of several men or women.

"26th Friday [November, 1779] Last night two Indians arrived from the Beaver River. They brought 50 made Beaver, 44 of which they would Trade for nothing but Brandy, The other 6 They traded for Ice Chissels & Hatchets . . . " [*Cumberland and Hudson House Journals, 1775–82*, Second Series, page 77.] One "made beaver" was a unit of currency equal to one prime beaver pelt.

FIREARMS—FRENCH AND ENGLISH

Figure 3

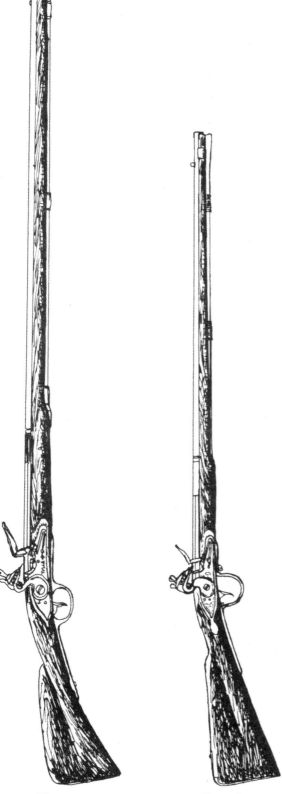

It is easy to understand why the Europeans were reluctant, at first, to furnish the Indians with firearms, for fear they might be turned against them. It was not long, however, before the traders realized that the firearm would provide the Indian with a more effective means of gathering fur and food. Eventually, guns began to flow to the natives who, in turn, often used them against their traditional enemies.

Figure 1 Fusil de chasse de Tulle, Modile de 1729–1734, from Russell Bouchard, *Les Fusils de Tulle en Nouvelle-France: 1691–1741*, page 68. "There were two distinct kinds of guns given or traded to the Indians by the French: the *fusil de traite* [trade gun] and the *fusil de chasse* [hunting gun]." [T. M. Hamilton, *Colonial Frontier Guns*, [page 31.]

Figure 2 An 1836 Barnett Hudson's Bay Company gun in the collections of the Museum of the Fur Trade, Chadron, Nebraska. [Courtesy of Charles E. Hanson, Jr.]

Figure 3 Tombstone fox on the lockplate of the H. B. C. gun illustrated in Figure 2. "By 1800, the encircled sitting fox stamped on the lockplate just below the pan was associated with the North West Company while a fox in an impressed cartouche was used by the H. B. C. Twenty-one years later, with the reorganization of the H. B. C. and its merger with the North West Company, a new fox, seated still, but facing left over the initials E. B. made its appearance." [James D. Forman, "Guns of the American Indians" in *The Canadian Journal of Arms Collecting*, Vol. II, No. 4, page 107.]

Figure 1

Figure 2

THE NORTHWEST GUN

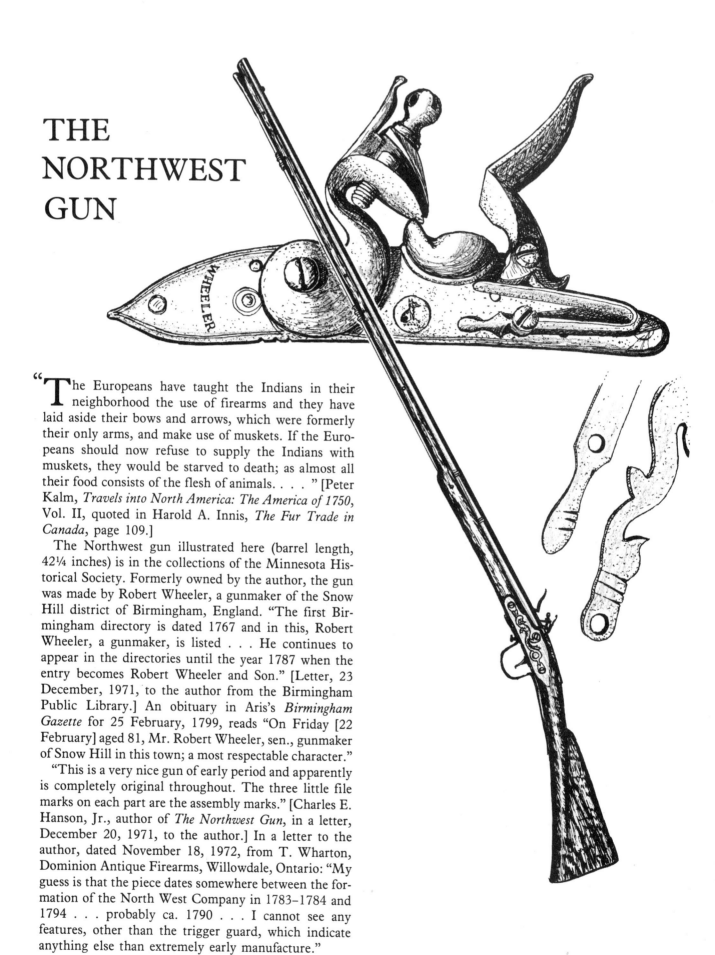

"The Europeans have taught the Indians in their neighborhood the use of firearms and they have laid aside their bows and arrows, which were formerly their only arms, and make use of muskets. If the Europeans should now refuse to supply the Indians with muskets, they would be starved to death; as almost all their food consists of the flesh of animals. . . . " [Peter Kalm, *Travels into North America: The America of 1750*, Vol. II, quoted in Harold A. Innis, *The Fur Trade in Canada*, page 109.]

The Northwest gun illustrated here (barrel length, 42¼ inches) is in the collections of the Minnesota Historical Society. Formerly owned by the author, the gun was made by Robert Wheeler, a gunmaker of the Snow Hill district of Birmingham, England. "The first Birmingham directory is dated 1767 and in this, Robert Wheeler, a gunmaker, is listed . . . He continues to appear in the directories until the year 1787 when the entry becomes Robert Wheeler and Son." [Letter, 23 December, 1971, to the author from the Birmingham Public Library.] An obituary in Aris's *Birmingham Gazette* for 25 February, 1799, reads "On Friday [22 February] aged 81, Mr. Robert Wheeler, sen., gunmaker of Snow Hill in this town; a most respectable character."

"This is a very nice gun of early period and apparently is completely original throughout. The three little file marks on each part are the assembly marks." [Charles E. Hanson, Jr., author of *The Northwest Gun*, in a letter, December 20, 1971, to the author.] In a letter to the author, dated November 18, 1972, from T. Wharton, Dominion Antique Firearms, Willowdale, Ontario: "My guess is that the piece dates somewhere between the formation of the North West Company in 1783–1784 and 1794 . . . probably ca. 1790 . . . I cannot see any features, other than the trigger guard, which indicate anything else than extremely early manufacture."

GUNFLINTS, GUNWORMS, AND SHOT

It wasn't only a matter of supplying guns to the Indians, for to be of any use, each required gun powder, balls, and shot of different sizes (depending on game or fowl to be killed), flints, and gun worms used to withdraw a charge from the barrel.

Figure 1 X-ray of upper portion of gun barrel recovered from the Granite River in 1962. Note the multiple shot still in the barrel. In almost every case where individual muskets were recovered from underwater, they were loaded with multiple shot. Game was often scarce along the well-travelled routes, and every canoe carried one or two guns loaded. Multiple shot, of a larger size, improved the hunter's chances on some game as well as waterfowl.

Figure 2 "Gun powder had to be accompanied by shot of some variety if it were to be of any use, and many kinds of shot are mentioned in the Merchants' account books: royal shot, duck shot, pigeon shot, etc., are frequently mentioned." [Marie Gérin-Lajoie and Kenneth Kidd, "Montreal Merchants' Records," mimeographed.]

Figure 3 Gun worm excavated at the 1802–1803 Yellow River post in Wisconsin. Gun worms were necessary to remove or unload a charged musket. There were often times when the hunter, with musket loaded with shot, came upon a large animal like a moose, deer or bear, and it was necessary to change to a ball.

Figure 4 The gunflint was held firmly in the cock or hammer, and when the trigger was pulled, the flint struck the frizzen, causing sparks to ignite the powder in the pan. The fire travelled through the touch hole igniting the powder in the barrel, thus firing the piece. "Flints French, is noways pleasing to Indians, they being for the most part very unshapable for a gun." [*Letters from Hudson Bay, 1703–1740*, Vol. XXV, page 279.]

Letter 72 from James Isham at York Fort, dated 20 July, 1739, stated defects in certain trade goods as reported by Indians: "Gunworms is very unhandy, being short and too wide for a ramrod, they being obliged to put a piece of paper round the ramrod before the worm will be fast, by which reason they lose many a deer etc. before they have time to draw the small shot to put a ball in." [*Letters from Hudson Bay, 1703–40*, page 279.]

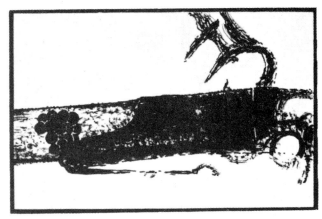

Figure 1

Figure 4

Lead musket balls and shot in great numbers were recovered by divers of the Quetico-Superior Project. [Illustration adapted from underwater photo taken by Joseph Jabas. Gunflints and shot from the collections of the Minnesota Historical Society.]

CROSSES OF SILVER

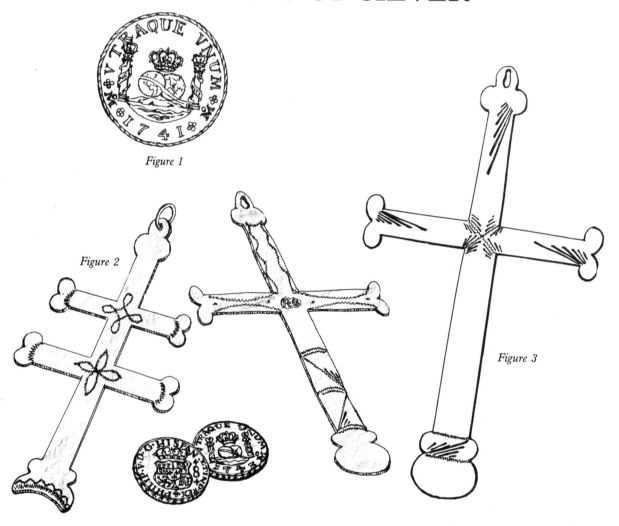

Figure 1

Figure 2

Figure 3

Colorful beads, dyed quills, feathers, shells, paint, and other items of decoration and adornment were frequently used to bargain with the Indians. When metal jewelry became available in the form of brooches, gorgets, armbands, necklaces, rings, and crosses, it achieved great popularity with them.

"The cross was introduced in North America by Christian missionaries who gave crosses of copper and brass (rarely of silver) to their Indian converts. It quickly achieved secular popularity, and was manufactured in large quantities for the fur trade." [N. Jaye Fredrickson, *The Covenant Chain*, page 61.]

Figure 1 An important source of silver for the 17th and 18th-century silversmith was the Spanish rials or pieces of eight. The coin illustrated here was recovered by divers from the Hollandia wreck, 1743, a Dutch East Indiaman, off the English coast. Before 1732 such coins

were clipped to the correct weight and were known as cobs, but in that year the Spaniards installed a screw press in Mexico City to turn out round coins of exact weight. Diameter of coin, 1½ inches.

Figure 2 Lorraine cross. Maker unknown. Size, 5 inches high by 2½ inches wide. [Original in McCord Museum, McGill University, Montreal.]

Figure 3 Latin cross made by Robert Cruickshank of Montreal (1767–1809). Found at Big Sandy Lake, Minnesota, by Mr. and Mrs. Clifford Olson and presented to the Minnesota Historical Society. Size, 5 inches high by 2¾ inches wide.

Among the artifacts recovered from an Indian grave, thought to be that of Chief Little Turtle, at Fort Wayne during a construction project, were silver bracelets, anklets, medals, crosses, ear rings, pendants, and brooches.

70

BROOCHES AND BEAVERS OF SILVER

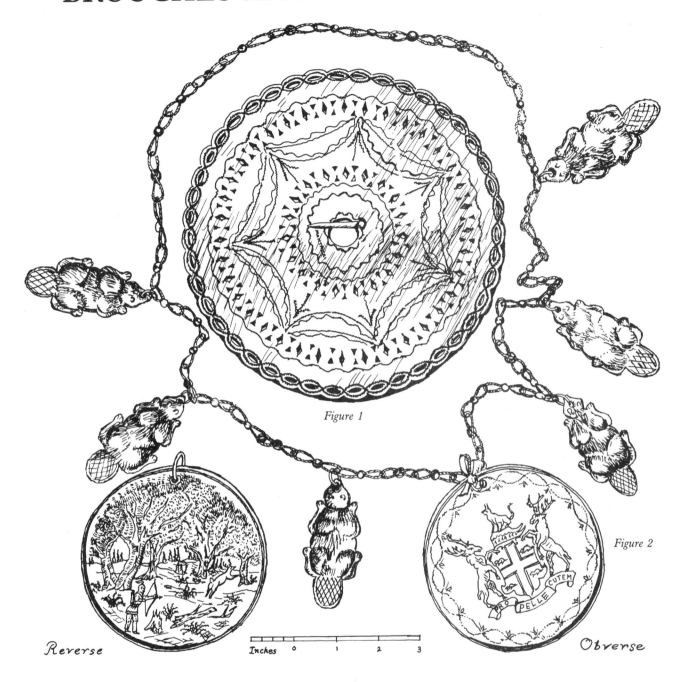

Figure 1

Reverse   Inches 0 1 2 3   Obverse

Figure 2

Figure 1 German silver round brooch marked MONTREAL. Maker unknown. Size, 7¾ inches in diameter. [Original in the McCord Museum, McGill University, Montreal.] "1775—Destination: Michilimackinac, Bale No. 31, 6 pairs Glass beads, bracelets, 12 Necklaces, 12 Shells, 2000 Silver brooches, one case containing 6 North guns and 2 ordinary." [Marie Gérin-Lajoie and Kenneth Kidd, "Montreal Merchants' Records," mimeographed.]

Figure 2 Round, sterling-silver medal with the Hudson's Bay Company coat-of-arms engraved on the front. The medal is suspended from an unusual chain bearing six sterling-silver beavers. There is some suspicion that this may not be an authentic fur-trade period piece. [From the collection of Kenneth O. Leonard, South Dakota.]

SILVER ARMBAND

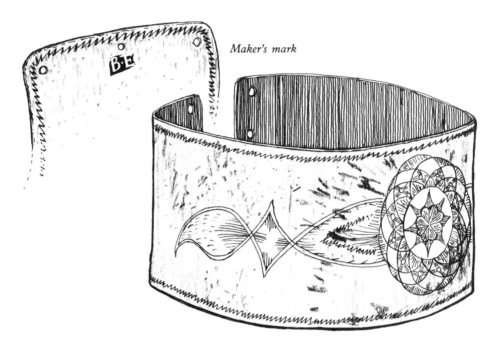

Maker's mark

Silver armband found at Petite Faucille Rapids on the Voyageurs' Channel of the French River in 1972. Circumference, 10¼ inches. Height, 1 15/16 inches. Diameter, 3 5/16 inches. [Original in the National Museum of Man, Ottawa, Canada.]

This silver-plated armband is marked "B E" for Benjamin Etter, 1763-1827, a silversmith in Halifax, Nova Scotia, who worked between 1787 and 1813. The armband was recovered, along with other trade goods, by the 1711 Underwater Archaeological Society, Guelph, Ontario. Dr. Walter A. Kenyon, former associate curator of archaeology, Royal Ontario Museum, and members of the staff of the Ontario Department of Lands and Forests, were highly successful in their underwater search of the rapids on the French River in the 1960's

and 70's. The French River, which flows westward between Lake Nipissing and Georgian Bay, was an important link in the main trade route between Montreal and the western posts. Literally all the canoe brigades bound for Michilimackinac, Green Bay, the Mississippi, Grand Portage, Fond du Lac, Folle Avoine, and other western posts passed down this river. With its several bad rapids and the direction of flow westward – right for the movement of trade goods – it proved to be the most productive of all waterways for the recovery of fur-trade artifacts.

Fur trader Peter Grant, in describing the natives, states, "They wear silver bracelets, either on the naked arm or over the sleeve of the coat." [L. R. Masson, *Les Bourgeois de la Compagnie du Nord-Ouest*, page 316.]

STONEWARE AND PLAYING CARDS

Figure 1

Figure 2

The types and kinds of merchandise, which were imported from Europe for trade in North America, were many and varied. One ordinarily thinks of beads, axes, kettles, guns, and knives, but the inventories also listed such things as handkerchiefs, sleeves, shirts, hats, and even playing cards. Cards were undoubtedly popular, for over a long period of time, great quantities of playing cards appeared along with other merchandise destined for distant posts. Also brought into the interior were exquisite vases, glassware, plates, and other ceramics, for the most part for traders, but some reached the natives—witness the Tunica Treasure.

Figure 1 Vase of gray, salt-glazed stoneware (Wester-

wald) from the graves of the Tunica Indians, eighteenth-century middlemen in the lower Mississippi River fur trade. GR medallions were used to ornament some of the Westerwald export during the eighteenth century. "GR" stood for Georgius Rex, referring to George I or George II of England. [Adapted from Jeffrey P. Brain, *Tunica Treasure*, Peabody Museum Papers, copyright 1979 by the President and Fellows of Harvard College.]

Figure 2 Early nineteenth-century French playing cards in the collections of the McCord Museum, McGill University, Montreal. Playing cards frequently appeared on the inventories of goods sent to the interior posts. The Montreal merchant, Monière, in his first journal dated May 24, 1724, listed among items a spring outfit destined for Green Bay, 12 bales of trade goods and "48 decks of playing cards." [Marie Gérin-Lajoie and Kenneth Kidd, "Montreal Merchants' Records," mimeographed.]

The date of the playing cards illustrated is uncertain: "We have a pack dated 1827, which are unusual because they are double heads. Most cards have the full-length figures until a considerably later date." [Catherine Perry Hargrave, *A History of Playing Cards and a Bibliography of Cards and Gaming,* page 57.]

****

On contact with the Europeans the Indian's culture began to change. With the introduction of the white man's goods, old Indian ways commenced to disappear, but not at the rate many have believed. It is now known that frequently the Indian made use of certain trade items in ways other than the purpose for which they were intended. For example, kettles, guns, knives, etc., were often buried with the dead, and lead and certain metals were melted into decorative shapes and pieces. It is also known that some tribes refused to accept all of the white man's innovations. The bow and arrow was sometimes preferred over the gun for killing buffalo.

The records of the Hudson's Bay Company have revealed that the Indian, in numerous instances, did not accept the white man's items as they were introduced. The natives frequently demanded alterations to guns, axes, kettles, and other goods before they would accept them.

The Rendezvous

"As this [Grand Portage] is the Headquarters

of General Rendezvous for all who commerce in this

part of the World, therefore every Summer the Proprietors

and many of the Clerks who Winter in the Interior come

here with the furs . . . and I am told this is the time when

they generally arrive but some of them are already here.

Those who bring the goods from Montreal go no further

than this." [Daniel Williams Harmon, *A Journal of Voyages

and Travels in the Interior of North America*, pages 15-16.]

Grand Portage

LE GRAND PORTAGE

Le Grande Portage, or the "great carrying place;" was known to the Indians perhaps as long as 8,000 years before the coming of the white man. Archaeological evidence found on the Rainy River has revealed that ancestors of modern Indians have occupied the region since that time. There is no question that Indians have used the waters between Lake Superior and Lake of the Woods as a trade route for centuries. Tools fashioned from native Lake Superior copper have been found all along that water route. White man's use of the Pigeon River route is limited to a mere 250 years. The Pigeon, a relatively easy access to the Northwest, emptied into Lake Superior. However, in its last few miles, the river drops several hundred feet over a series of cascades and waterfalls before reaching the lake. The users of the route had to make an 8½-mile carry or portage to reach the navigable portion of the river. It was one of the longest portages on the North American continent, exceeded only by the thirteen-mile Methye Portage between Lac la Loche and the Clearwater River in northern Saskatchewan. In spite of the problems posed by the Grand Portage, it was preferred by the traders.

Searching for the Western Sea and a route to the interior, a member of the exploring and trading party of Pierre Gaultier de Varennes, Sieur de la Vérendrye, crossed the 8½-mile portage in 1731 to establish a post at Rainy Lake. From that point on, until 1803–1804, the portage was in almost constant use by the French and later the British traders. The artist's conception of the North West Company depot is based on the archaeological work conducted over the years for the Grand Portage National Monument, much of which was done by Alan R. Woolworth of the Minnesota Historical Society. The North West Company depot has been partially reconstructed and is open to the public.

Grand Portage was strategically located midway on the arc between Montreal and the rich beaver lands of the Athabasca country. Geographically, it was a key location, the portage being as far west as the huge freight canoes could easily travel. It was on the shores of Grand Portage Bay that the North West Company built its main depot, the scene of great activity when the business partners from Montreal, the great canoes, and the winterers from the interior, met and rendezvoused each July. John Macdonell, in his diary published in *Five Fur Traders of the Northwest*, page 94, leaves us a brief description of Grand Portage: "All the buildings within the Fort are sixteen in number made with cedar and white spruce fir split with whip saws after being suquared (*sic*) . . . " The scene depicted by the artist is of the 1802 period, although at that time there were sixteen buildings, not all of which have been excavated.

"The North West Company was the forerunner of confederation, and it was built on the work of the French voyageur, the contributions of the Indian, especially the canoe, Indian corn and pemmican, and the organizing ability of Anglo-American merchants." [Harold A. Innis, *The Fur Trade in Canada*, page 262.]

George Nelson, a clerk for the XY Company, left us this description of the activities at Grand Portage in 1802: "I was placed in one of the Stores to Serve the people. At last they began to come in, all was business. Receiving goods, corn, flour, pork, etc. from Montreal & Mackinac, & furs from the different wintering posts—Gambling, feasting, dancing, drinking & fighting. After a couple of weeks to rest, for the Winterers to give in their returns & accounts, & to make up their outfits, they began to return again, to run over the same ground, toils, labors, and dangers." [Erwin N. Thompson, *Grand Portage: The Great Carrying Place*, page 109.]

FORT WILLIAM ON THE KAMINISTIQUIA

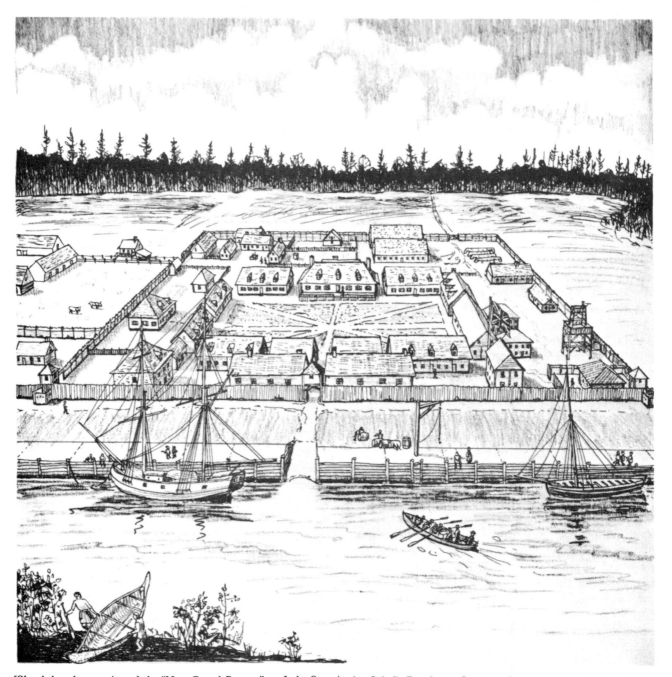

[Sketch based on a view of the "New Grand Portage" on Lake Superior by Col. J. Bouchette. Courtesy, Public Archives of Canada.]

Fort William, on the Kaministiquia River, was built by the North West Company between 1801 and 1807, after the border between the United States and Canada had been established at the Pigeon River as a result of the 1783 Treaty of Paris.

Named for William McGillivray, chief superintendent of the North West Company, the fort served as the Company's headquarters from 1803 to 1821 when it merged with its rival, the Hudson's Bay Company.

From that point on, Fort William declined in importance. The Kaministiquia route was known and used by the French traders long before Grand Portage. By the early 1700's, however, the northern trail was all but forgotten in favor of the shorter and easier Pigeon River route via the Grand Portage. Today the Old Fort William complex has been reconstructed and is open to the public.

SPIRITS IN BOTTLES

Figure 2

Most of the liquor—rum and brandy—brought in by the traders was carried in kegs and barrels. The imported wines, on the other hand, were carried in bottles and often in the cassettes of the traders. The appearance of wine and liquor bottles on a site would suggest the presence of more refined beverages intended for white or European consumption. "It is not difficult to interpret such archaeological finds as bottles, glasses, and spigots. The evidence all indicates that the residents and visitors to Michilimackinac, as a group, were a hard-drinking lot, in an age noted for its extraordinarily heavy consumption of liquor . . . Rum and wine were poured freely at routine social events at the post." [Eugene T. Petersen., *Gentlemen on the Frontier: A Pictorial Record of Michilimackinac*, page 26.]

Figure 1 Blue-green case bottle found underwater at Fort Charlotte in 1963. The bottle is similar to others recovered from French sites in the western Great Lakes area.

Figure 2 Dark olive-green, eighteenth-century English wine bottle recovered from the Pigeon River off Fort Charlotte. Height, 8½ inches.

Figure 3 Light olive-green wine bottle fragment, probably of eighteenth-century origin, recovered at Fort Charlotte. [Bottles from the Minnesota Historical Society collection.]

"An Indian will barter away all his furs, may even leave himself without a rag to cover his nakedness, in exchange for that vile unwholesome stuff called English brandy." [Edward Umfreville, *The Present State of Hudson's Bay*, page 16.]

The Belongings

Ile à la Crosse,

1 October. 1787

Dear Roderic,

. . . I put your Books all but the History of England

into your Cassette. I have no necessaries to send you. You

will pass the winter in the best manner you can . . .

I remain Dear Roderic

Yours sincerely

A. Mackenzie

CANOE CUPS

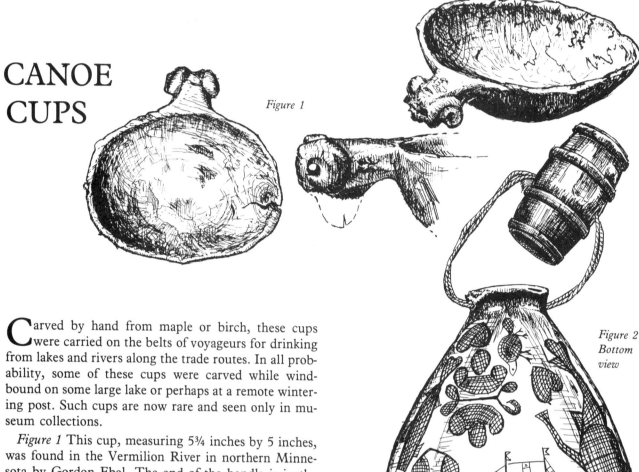

Figure 1

*Figure 2
Bottom
view*

Carved by hand from maple or birch, these cups were carried on the belts of voyageurs for drinking from lakes and rivers along the trade routes. In all probability, some of these cups were carved while windbound on some large lake or perhaps at a remote wintering post. Such cups are now rare and seen only in museum collections.

Figure 1 This cup, measuring 5¾ inches by 5 inches, was found in the Vermilion River in northern Minnesota by Gordon Ebel. The end of the handle is in the form of the head of a Rocky Mountain Big Horn sheep. Ebel, a game warden, found the cup protruding from the mud several miles below a bad rapids and waterfall where it probably had become lodged after floating downstream. Buried in the mud for well over two centuries, the cup is remarkably well preserved. It seems likely that the carver, some French voyageur or Indian canoeman, had seen the Big Horn sheep in the Rocky Mountains.

Figure 2 This cup, highly decorated with incised flowers, hearts, a ship, a beaver, a mermaid, fish, four-leaf clover and a snake, is from the early nineteenth century. It measures 4¾ long by 3⅛ wide by 1¾ inches deep. [Price Collection, Canadian Centre for Folk Culture Studies, National Museum of Man, Ottawa. Adapted from photo by Robert Filion, National Museum of Canada.]

Figure 3 Abenaki burl drinking cup made of rock maple, 1807. [Courtesy, McCord Museum, McGill University, Montreal.]

"Wooden canoe cups were personal utensils of the voyageurs for scooping a quick drink of water over the gunwale or for ladling sagamite from the communal cauldron. Whittled by their owners on stormy days or at night around the campfire, some of the canoe cups became works of folk art . . . " [Kenneth G. Roberts and Philip Shackleton, *The Canoe*, page 192.]

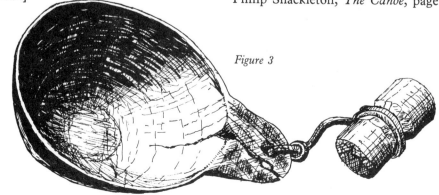

Figure 3

PIPES, PORRINGERS, AND SNUFF MILLS

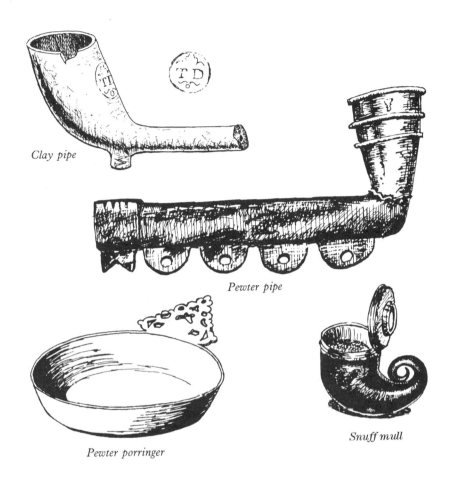

Clay pipe

Pewter pipe

Pewter porringer

Snuff mull

Pewter porringers and other pewter artifacts were characteristic of the eighteenth century. The author was present at the site of Old Fort Albany on James Bay in 1963 when archaeologist Walter A. Kenyon, of the Royal Ontario Museum, unearthed the handle of a pewter porringer similar to that illustrated here. It carried the date 1707. Fort Albany was one of the earliest Hudson's Bay Company posts.

The pewter pipe illustrated on this page was recovered by divers of the Minnesota Historical Society in August, 1961, from a rapids on the Basswood River. The river forms a portion of the Minnesota-Ontario border and a link in the main Grand Portage-Lake Winnipeg route. This rare pipe of European manufacture was found with a number of other trade items including axes, knives, beads, ice chisels, spears, musket balls, shot, and vermilion paint. Its discovery was fortunate as it was found in two pieces some ten feet apart. Burned tobacco was still caked in the bowl after almost two hundred years. The four perforated flanges on the under side of the stem were designed for feathers or other dec-

orations. This item would likely have been traded without the customary long wooden stem. The cast pewter pipe measures 4½ inches in length. [Minnesota Historical Society collection.]

The horn snuff mill illustrated was the property of trader Henry McKenzie, younger brother of Roderic McKenzie. In 1803 he was at Fort William and in 1815 was elected a member of the Beaver Club in Montreal. [Courtesy, Nor'Westers and Loyalist Museum, Williamstown, Ontario.]

The clay pipe illustrated was found at Horsetail Rapids on the Granite River by divers of the Quetico-Superior Project. Clay pipes, like beads and bottles, are considered by historical archaeologists to be an important diagnostic key to a period in history. The shape, size, and marking of this example, according to Iain Walker's *Clay Tobacco Pipes, With Particular Reference to the Bristol Industry*, Volume 4, page 1527, points to a 1760–1800 period of manufacture. [Minnesota Historical Society collection.]

CASSETTES

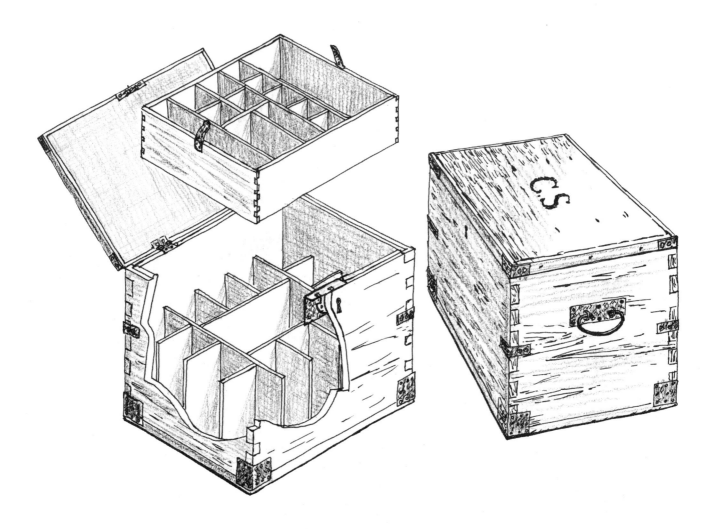

The term "*cassette*" is French for small box, and during the fur-trade period this could mean any sort of carrying case used to secure small articles as distinguished from the large packs, sacks, bales, or "pieces" which made up most of the load. Cassettes were used to carry the personal effects or property of the traders—for example, medicines, books, bottles of wine or gin, scissors, writing materials, and eating utensils.

The *cassette* illustrated here belonged to fur trader Charles Stewart (1820–1907). Lined with green cloth, it had bottom tiers which seem to have been designed to carry "case bottles" of liquor. Length, 21⅝ by 15½ wide by 14¼ inches deep. [Original in the Nor'Westers & Loyalist Museum, Williamstown, Ontario.]

"About 1847 James Cameron was joined at Timiskaming by his cousin Charles Stewart . . . About 1851, Charles Stewart was advanced to the rank of clerk, and in 1868 he was placed in charge at Timiskaming House, with the rank of Chief Trader." [W. Stewart Wallace, *The Pedlars from Quebec and Other Papers on the Nor'Westers*, page 90.]

"In 1743 Pierre Guy senior purchased a quantity of locks for small chests from Havy and Lefebvre, whose sales in Quebec, included 2½ dozen of 3 inch, 3 dozen of 2½ inch, 4 dozen of 2 inch, and 2 dozen of 1¾ inch. It was specified that they were all for small chests (cassettes)." [Marie Gérin-Lajoie and Kenneth Kidd, "Montreal Merchants' Records," mimeographed.]

THE MCGILLIVRAY PISTOL

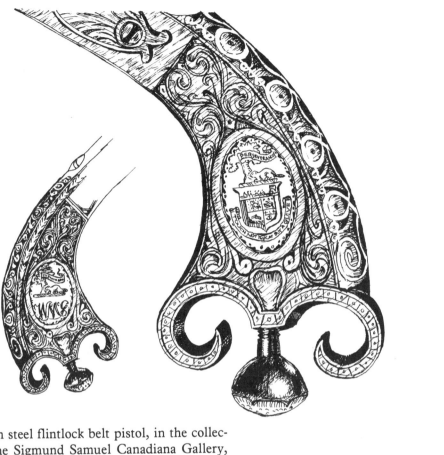

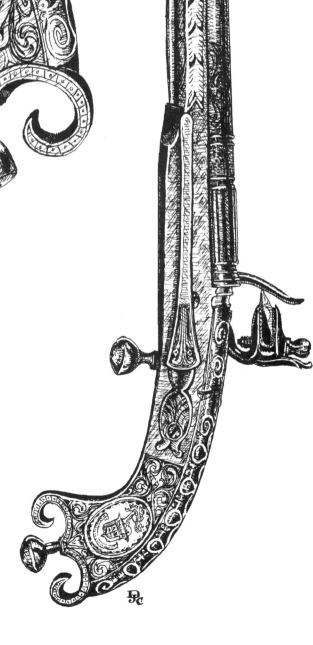

The Scottish steel flintlock belt pistol, in the collections of the Sigmund Samuel Canadiana Gallery, Royal Ontario Museum, Toronto, was the property of William McGillivray, one of the most influential partners of the North West Company. Fort William was named after him in 1807. The pistol was made by John Murdoch, of Doune, between 1770–1785. It was probably a presentation piece. An oval silver escutcheon on the left side of the butt is engraved with the arms of William McGillivray. On the right escutcheon is engraved a design similar to the North West Company seal—a beaver gnawing on a tree and the motto PERSEVERANCE.

The motto engraved under the McGillivray family crest reads "Touch Not The Cat But the Glove." It is generally understood as meaning "Touch not the cat unless you are wearing a glove." [Robert and George MacGillivray, *A History of the Clan McGillivray*, page 173.]

See also Major John Pitcairn's pair of ornate Scottish pistols (eighteenth century) made by John Murdoch, and illustrated in M. L. Brown's *Firearms in Colonial America, 1492–1792*, page 300. The Pitcairn pistols are almost identical to the McGillivray pistol. Major Pitcairn was the British officer commanding at Lexington and Concord.

NEW ITEMS FROM OLD MERCHANDISE

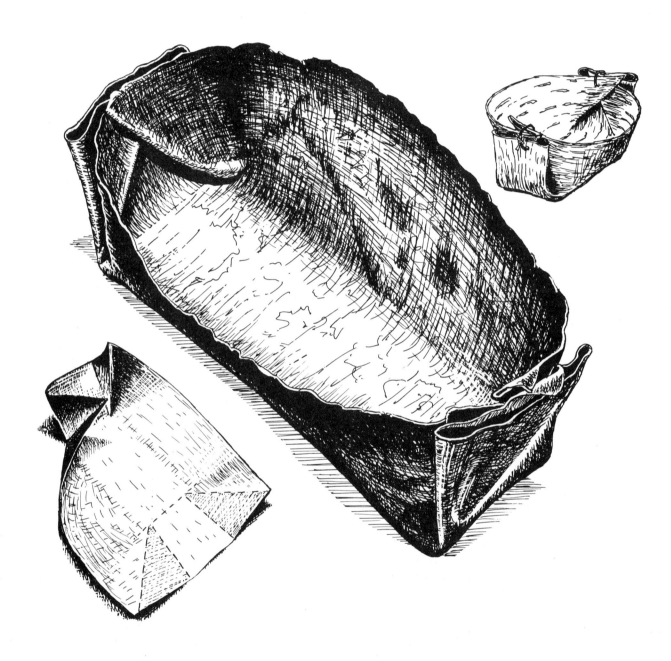

The copper vessel illustrated on this page was found on a portage along the Minnesota-Ontario border by Gary Hokkanen, a guide in the early 1970's. Made by an Indian from a discarded kettle, it illustrates how the natives re-used discarded items of trade. Knives were fashioned from worn-out files, and gun barrels were often converted to fleshers for removing fat from hides. Artist David Christofferson sketches an Indian-made bark dish in the upper right-hand corner to show graphically the similarity between it and the copper vessel. The copper artifact measures 7¾ inches in length, 4½ inches in width, and 2½ inches in depth. The sketch at the lower left illustrates the method used by the natives to fold the bark or copper to fashion a water-tight container.

RAMSAY CROOK'S BUCKSKIN JACKET AND LEGGINGS

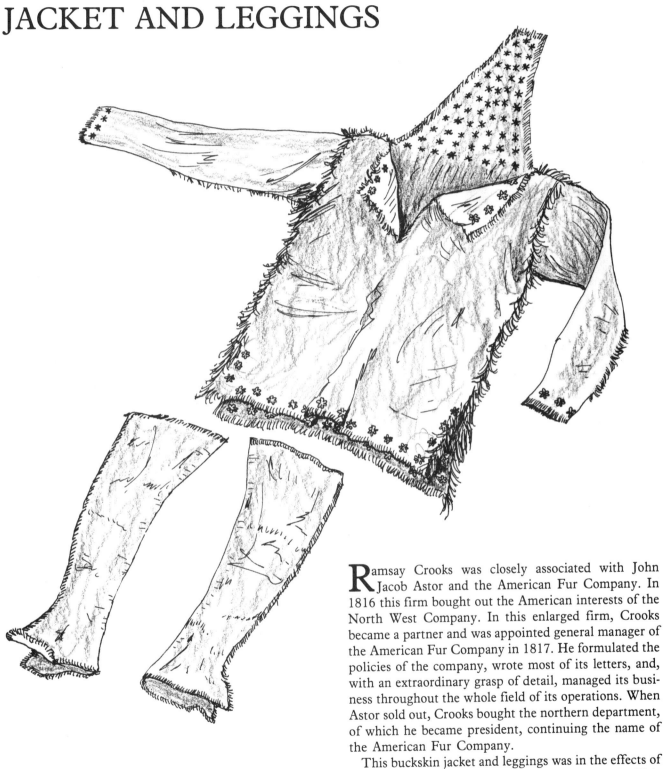

Ramsay Crooks was closely associated with John Jacob Astor and the American Fur Company. In 1816 this firm bought out the American interests of the North West Company. In this enlarged firm, Crooks became a partner and was appointed general manager of the American Fur Company in 1817. He formulated the policies of the company, wrote most of its letters, and, with an extraordinary grasp of detail, managed its business throughout the whole field of its operations. When Astor sold out, Crooks bought the northern department, of which he became president, continuing the name of the American Fur Company.

This buckskin jacket and leggings was in the effects of Ramsay Crooks, who brought it back from Astoria. This is fully documented by its present owner, Warren Baker of Montreal.

BEAVER CLUB MEDAL AND CUTLERY BOX

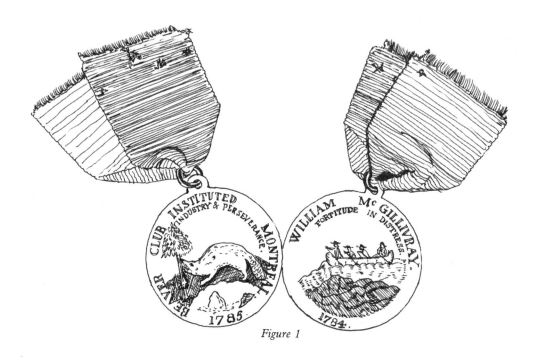

Figure 1

The Nor'Westers, called "the master pedlars" by their rivals, did things in style. Social lords of Montreal as well as the town's business leaders, they organized the famous Beaver Club, an attempt to weld together a somewhat odd mixture of fur traders. When the club was founded in 1785, only men who had wintered in *le pays d'en haut*, or upper country, could qualify as members. On admission each member was obligated to have a gold medal made, properly engraved with his name and the date of his first visit to the Indian country, and to wear it on a blue ribbon at every meeting.

Figure 1 William McGillivray Beaver Club medal. Diameter, 1½ inches. [From the original work, Glenbow Museum, Calgary, Alberta, Canada.]

Figure 2 The Beaver Club cutlery box, carrying the date 1815, was used to store the Club's silver. The beautifully crafted box measures 19½ x 10⅜ x 3¾ inches. [Warren Baker collection, Montreal, Canada.]

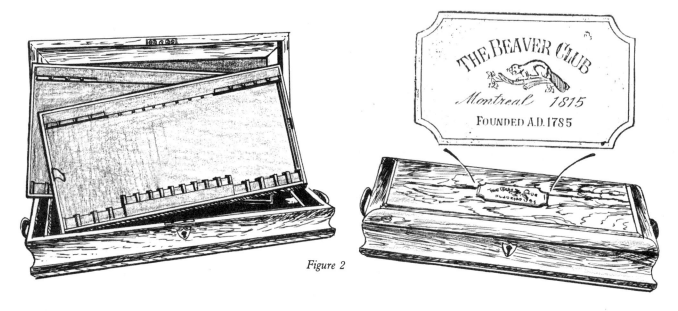

Figure 2

The Surprise—
Amenities
in the Wilderness

"In 1803 Daniel Williams Harmon, writing from
the North West Company's post at Fort Alexandria in the
Swan River District, lamented the fact that he would be
virtually alone for the summer. 'However fortunately for me
I have dead Friends (my books) who will never abandon me,
till I first neglect them." [*The Beaver*, Spring, 1983, page 44.]

FAIENCE PLATES

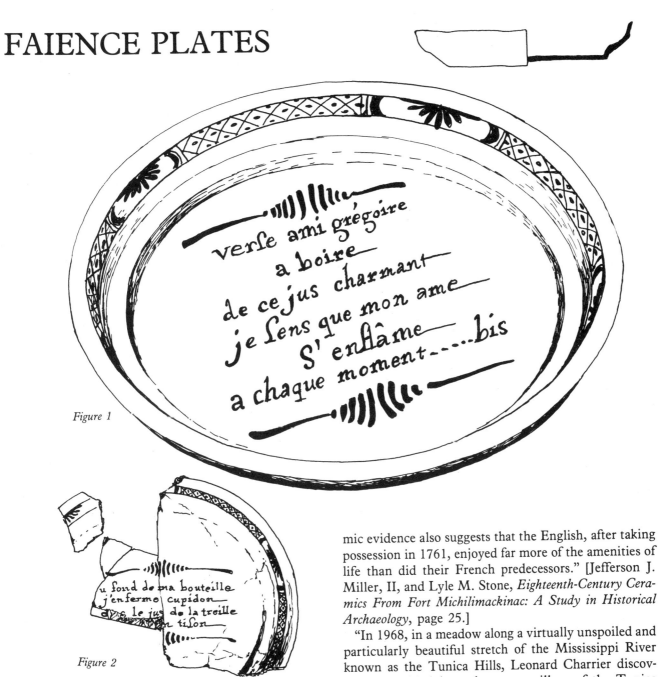

Figure 1

Figure 2

Although the French and English traders, the upper class of the fur trade, lived beyond the limits of civilization, it is known through historical documentation and archaeology that they often took a few of the finer things of life with them—for example, silver utensils, clothing, shoes, shoe buckles, books, imported wines, crystal glasses, vases, and fine china. "The ceramic evidence also suggests that the English, after taking possession in 1761, enjoyed far more of the amenities of life than did their French predecessors." [Jefferson J. Miller, II, and Lyle M. Stone, *Eighteenth-Century Ceramics From Fort Michilimackinac: A Study in Historical Archaeology*, page 25.]

"In 1968, in a meadow along a virtually unspoiled and particularly beautiful stretch of the Mississippi River known as the Tunica Hills, Leonard Charrier discovered the mid-eighteenth-century village of the Tunica Indians and unearthed a collection of artifacts unmatched in North America as a record of the contact between the natives of the continent and the French." [*The New Yorker*, July 27, 1981, page 41.] Among the countless artifacts was this complete blue and white *faience* plate (Figure 1), 8⅛ inches in diameter and 1 7/16 inches high. The inscription reads, "Serve friend Gregory to drink of this charming juice I feel that my soul is inflamed at each moment . . . again." The design on the plate indicates it was manufactured in either Rouen or Nevers, France. [Adapted from Jeffrey P. Brain, *Tunica Treasure*, Peabody Museum Papers, Vol. 71,

The blue and white *faience* plate illustrated in Figure 2, virtually identical in treatment to that in Figure 1 (except for the inscription), was found in the water at Fort Charlotte by archaeologist Douglas Birk of the Minnesota Historical Society. The inscription reads, "At the bottom of my bottle I imprison love, for the juice of the grape makes my heart burn with passion." [Wheeler, et al., *Voices from the Rapids*, page 89.]

A SET OF TIN DISHES

Three of a nest of eighteen tin dishes recovered from the Winnipeg River by the Quetico-Superior Underwater Research Project divers. On the bottom of the dishes is marked the name of the maker, Townsend & Compton. [Royal Ontario Museum collection.]

Historical research in the journals and diaries of traders had revealed an accident which had occurred to the canoe brigade of Alexander Henry the Younger on August 9, 1800. Henry, leaving Grand Portage on July 19 bound for Lake Winnipeg, was following the usual route which, according to the trader, was "too well known to require description." [*The Manuscript Journals of Alexander Henry and David Thompson, 1799–1814*, Vol. I, page 6.] At Portage de l'Isle, the fatal wreck site, one of his canoes, in order to avoid the portage, passed down near the north shore with a full load. The loss amounted to five bales of merchandise, two bales of new tobacco, one bale canal tobacco, one bale kettles, one bale balls, one bale shot, and one case of guns. In this accident one man was lost. The tin dishes illustrated were not a part of Henry's cargo, as the Townsend & Compton firm began operation in London a year later in 1801. Traders have reported many accidents at that location, so recoveries there could be described as an archaeological omelet.

"No tablecloth shed its snowy whiteness over the board; no silver candelabra or gaudy china interfered with its simple magnificence. The bright tin plates and dishes reflected jolly faces, and burnished gold can give no finer zest to a feast." [Paul Kane, *Wanderings of an Artist*, page 262.]

Accidents
in the Fur Trade

In the late summer of 1960, a chance find by divers in northern Minnesota of a rare nest of seventeen brass trade kettles set in motion an international project involving the Minnesota Historical Society and the Royal Ontario Museum. Its purpose was to conduct an underwater search along the main fur-trade route for materials relating to that early trade. During a thirteen-year period, countless objects were recovered, a number of which are illustrated in this book.

For the first several years, the search efforts were conducted at rapids and waterfalls where accidents might have occurred. The obvious danger spots were not always the productive ones. The milder rapids, which would tempt the voyageurs to run, more often paid the higher dividends in recovered goods. It was also discovered that the westward-flowing rivers were the ones to be searched as they carried the trade goods. Goods moving westward would also travel up eastward-flowing streams; however, in such cases accidents were less likely to occur. Here it would involve lining a canoe or poling. It became very evident that the most productive rivers were those which not only flowed westward but carried a higher percentage of traffic – for example, the French River in Ontario.

Accidents were of several types. First, and perhaps foremost, were those which occurred during attempts to run a rapids, where the loss involved goods, life, or both. Secondly were the accidents on the larger lakes when the canoes were under sail. Here again the losses could involve goods, life or both. Thirdly were those which occurred on the portages where the canoemen would slip and fall under a heavy load, either carrying packs or a canoe. Hernias were commonplace with the canoemen. Men, carrying heavy loads and wading waist deep in icy water, grew old at thirty-five. Lastly, an occasional accident happened lining or poling a canoe upstream where a line would break or a man would slip.

Following are a number of excerpts from the journals of traders. Although there were many accidents reported, few were of use to the modern searcher, as tra-ders seldom gave accurate information as to location. Alexander Henry the Younger was an exception.

"Aug. 9th [1800] . . . We were troubled by a thick fog, which caused us to lose much time in going round the bays. We at last got astray and were obliged to wait until the weather cleared up about ten o'clock, when we proceeded to Portage de l'Isle [on the Winnipeg River], about 50 paces over. One of my canoes, to avoid the trouble of making this portage, passed down near the N. shore with a full load. As my own canoe was soon over the portage, we loaded and embarked, and on pushing from shore I perceived the canoe on the N. side coming off to sault [shoot] the rapids. She had not gone many yards when, by some mismanagement of the foreman, the current bore down her bow full upon the shore, against a rock, upon which the fellow, taking advantage of this situation, jumped, whilst the current whirled the canoe around. The steersman, finding himself within reach of the shore, jumped upon the rock with one of the midmen; the other midman, not being sufficiently active, remained in the canoe, which was instantly carried out and lost to view amongst the high waves. At length she appeared and stood perpendicular for a moment, when she sank down again, and I then perceived the man riding upon a bale of dry goods in the midst of the waves. We made every exertion to get near him, and did not cease calling out to him to take courage and not let go his hold; but alas! he sank under a heavy swell, and when the bale arose the man appeared no more . . . The loss amounted to five bales of merchandise, two bales new tobacco, one bale canal tobacco, one bale kettles, one bale balls, one bale shot, one case guns . . . "
[*Manuscript Journals of Alexander Henry and David Thompson, 1799–1814*, Vol. I, pages 28–29.]

"After descending six miles further, we came to the last portage on the route to Slave Lake, which we crossed, and encamped in its lower end. It is called 'The Portage of the Drowned,' and it received that name from a melancholy accident which took place many years ago. Two canoes arrived at the upper end of the portage, in one of which there was an experienced guide. This man, judging from the height of the river, deemed it practicable to shoot the rapid, and determined upon trying it. He accordingly placed himself in the bow of his canoe, having previously agreed, that if the passage was found easy, he should, on reaching the bottom of the rapid, fire a musket, as a signal for the other canoe to follow. The rapid proved dangerous, and called for all the skill of the guide, and the utmost exertion of his crew, and they narrowly escaped destruction. Just as they were landing, an unfortunate fellow, seizing the loaded fowling piece, fired at a duck which rose at the instant. The guide, anticipating the consequences, ran with the utmost haste to the other end of the portage, but he was too late; the other canoe had pushed off, and he arrived only to witness the fate of his comrades. They got alarmed in the middle of the rapid, the canoe was upset, and every man perished." [Captain John Franklin, *Journey to the Shores of the Polar Sea, in 1819-20-21-22*, pages 129-131.]

"We hastened to get everything out of her, but my sugar and their molasses was damaged, but worse than all, my powder, which I immediately examined, was considerably damaged; I did not dare let the men know this last misfortune, as it would have discouraged them . . . " [L. R. Masson, *Les Bourgeois de la Compagnie du Nord-Ouest*, Vol. II, page 290.]

"One of our canoes fouled a stump, and tore two bits of bark from her bottom." [*Manuscript Journals of Alexander Henry and David Thompson, 1799-1814*, Vol. II, page 797.]

Lake Winnipeg, 1775. "I kept the north side of the lake and had not proceeded far before I was joined by Mr. Pond, a trader of some celebrity in the north-west. Next day, we encountered a severe gale, from the dangers of which we escaped, by making the island called the Buffalo's Head; but, not without the loss of a canoe and four men. The shores, from the entrance of this lake to the island, with exception of the points, are rocky and lofty: the points are rocky, but low. The wood is pine and fir." [Alexander Henry the Elder, *Travels and Adventures in Canada and the Indian Territories Between the Years 1760 and 1776*, pages 250-252.]

From the diary of John Macdonell, 1793: "A league below l'Enfant perdue under the high rocky ground and wood back of their encampment is a portage called le Grand Recolet where one of the North West Companys canoes manned by brothers of the name of Majeau [upset] and lost half the cargo about fifteen days ago. The few survivors and the goods that floated were picked [up] below the Rapid by the other canoes of the Brigade. These unfortunate men had made portage and loaded their canoe below it, but had neglected to put a man or two on shore with a bit of Line to stem the strong eddy which carried back to the fall, from a foolish coincidence in their own power, and in consequence were drawn down by the eddy under the pitch of the fall where the canoe instantly filled and sunk. Though some of the bodies were found far below this the seven crosses are erected here as a warning to others along with seven others in memory of former casualties." [*Five Fur Traders of the Northwest*, page 84.]

Winnipeg River. "At 'Barrière Portage' we found the black flies and mosquitoes so annoying all night, as to deprive us entirely of sleep. June 10th. — We ran three or four beautiful rapids today in our canoes, the men showing great expertness in their management, although so much risk attends it that several canoes have been lost in the attempt." [Paul Kane, *Wanderings of an Artist*, pages 45-46.]

Thursday, 15 [1800]. "Roche Capitaine Portage. This Portage is so named from a large rock, that rises to a considerable height above the water, in the middle of the rapid. During the day, we have come up several difficult ones, where many persons have drowned, either in coming up or going down. For every such unfortunate person, whether his corpse is found or not, a cross is erected by his companions, agreeably to a custom of the Roman Catholics; and at this place, I see no less than fourteen." [Daniel Williams Harmon, *A Journal of Voyages and Travels in the Interior of North America*, page 6.]

Charles Grant's report, dated April 24, 1780, described the problem: "The Indian Trade by every communication is carried on at great expense, labour and risk of both men and property; every year furnishes instances of the loss of men and goods by accident or otherwise." [Harold A. Innis, *The Fur Trade in Canada*, page 213.]

Letter from Alexander Mackenzie to the partners at Grand Portage, 15 February, 1789: "I had a very favorable voyage in to the country until a short distance from Ile à la Crosse when one of the canoes got injured and sunk. By this unfortunate accident I lost two men and eleven pieces of goods. After repairing the damages as well as we could, we continued our voyage and arrived at this department on the 29th September, which was our fifty-second day from Lac La Pluie and the shortest voyage, I believe, that has been performed to this quarter with loaded canoes." [L. R. Masson, *Les Bourgeois de la Compagnie du Nord-Ouest*, page 29.]

Winnipeg River, 1821, from the diary of Nicholas Garry: "Wednesday the 1st August. At 2 we embarked, at 5 we arrived at the Portage de l'Isle. This is a very dangerous Rapid, and so many fatal Accidents have attended the Sauting [shooting] of it that it has been interdicted to the Servants of both Companies. Our men forgetting Orders and wishing to avoid the Trouble of carrying the Canoe run it and we escaped, though an Absolution of Sin in a severe Ducking would not have justified this Rashness. The Danger of this Rapid had been mentioned to me but I had forgotten it." [*Proceedings and Transactions of the Royal Society of Canada*, Second Series, Vol. VI, page 129.]

Jean Perrault narrative, 1786: "We set out with a Party of four Canoes . . . We were heavily loaded, and could not travel with a high wind. We were compelled to Camp at pointe aux chenes 5 Leagues from mackinac, and we went on the next day, with the wind at our backs, which increased more and more until we were obliged To enter into the rivière de minagokes. We left our canoes at the entrance, in order to Continue on our way if the wind moderated, but it increased more and more. Then the men whiled away their time at Cards. . . . one of the men named Ste. germain entered the tent. He told us that a canoe had appeared under sail, coming from mackinac which could be seen only from time to time. For the lake was White As a sheet. Mr. laframboise arose, and said it could only be mr. paterson who would sàil in such a wind. Finally he doubled the point of the River. We met him on the beach. 'The east wind is very strong,' he said, 'but as I have only half a Load I can take advantage of it.' a man named Laporte, an old voyageur told him that there was danger as the Canoe Was quite loaded, that they had Had many people also, which was true. He had seven men, his interpreter, His servant, himself, and his Slave, Making in all eleven persons, with a great White dog . . . He determined to go on, in spite of the remonstrances we made (as well as His men). There were Two, Namely, Laporte, and his servant, whom he forced to embark. . . . They started in spite of us, and bore off to catch the wind, and we re-entered our tents. Some of the men remained to Watch them for The space of 20 minutes at the most, and as soon as they could see neither canoe nor sail, mr. laframboise took his Telescope, and saw with the rest of us, some debris of the canoe on The water, moved by the waves, which Confirmed our belief that they Had perished. . . . The wind fell in the night, and the lake was still very rough, nevertheless, the two other canoes remaining behind. . . . when we were some little Distance from the islands, we discovered The Casks and the bales, and then men that the waves had cast here and there Along the beach. We Disembarked As soon as we arrived, and our first Care was to draw in the Bodies which were rolling in the waves. . . . Mr. patersonne Was the Farthest away holding His panise [slave woman] by his hand, both half buried in the sand, and his dog Crouched beside them on the beach. When we undertook to Remove them from the beach, the dog

interfered. It was necessary to strike him, in order to approach them." [*Michigan Pioneer & Historical Collections*, Vol. XXXVII, pages 539–540.]

"On my return I found the canoes had arrived, and the people were busy carrying the baggage over the portage. This is upward of a mile long, but would be a very good road, were it not that the H.B Co. from York Factory, with large boats, are in the habit of laying down a succession of logs from one end to the other for the purpose of rolling their boats over. This is a nuisance to our people, frequently causing accidents which endanger their lives." [*Manuscript Journals of Alexander Henry and David Thompson, 1799–1814*, Vol. II, page 463.]

"This is a treacherous little lake when the wind is thus from below, there being a current which, when counteracted by the wind, causes a dangerous chopping sea; several instances are known of people throwing pieces overboard to save their lives. We were obliged to double-reef our sail before we got over, and then had a narrow escape from swamping. This lake is about two leagues across . . . " [*Manuscript Journals of Alexander Henry and David Thompson, 1799–1814*, Vol. II, page 464.]

"Just as we left the little [the Pack] River and entered the large [the Parsnip], my canoe struck on a bank of gravel and gave such a jerk that the foreman fell and hurt his side against the maitre [gunwale]." [W. Kaye Lamb, ed., *Simon Fraser Letters and Journals, 1806–1808*, page 205.]

Winnipeg River: "After crossing one of these portages, we observed, with astonishment, a number of people on the next portage, La Cave, about pistol-shot distance from us. They proved to be Mr. Hughes, formerly partner of the North West Company; Mr. Berens, a member of Committee, and suite: they were painfully situated, in consequence of the loss of their bowsman, who, by missing a stroke with his pole, fell into the rapid, and as drowned: the steerman was saved with great difficulty." [*John McLean's Notes of a Twenty-five Years' Service in the Hudson's Bay Territory*, page 125.]

Churchill River, 1821: "At noon we landed at the Otter Portage, where the river ran with great velocity for half a mile, among large stones. Having carried across the principal part of the cargo, the people attempted to track the canoes along the edge of the rapid. With the first they succeeded, but the other, in which were the foreman and steersman, was overset and swept away by the current . . . One man had reached the bank, but no traces could be found of the foreman, Louis Saint Jean. . . . So early a disaster deeply affected the spirits of the Canadians, and their natural vivacity gave way to melancholy forebodings, while they erected a wooden cross in the rocks near the spot where their companion perished." [Captain John Franklin, *Journey to the Shores of the Polar Sea*, Vol. II, pages 101–103.]

Food and Drink

Those who labored hard in the canoes and on the portages required huge amounts of nutritious food to keep their human engines running. Although the traders out of Montreal took provisions, and the English on Hudson Bay were supplied by ship, both had to depend heavily upon the natives for food. From the Indians they obtained corn, oats (wild rice), maple sugar, and a variety of game and waterfowl—venison, moose, buffalo, geese, ducks and others. When at a wintering post along a lake or river, fish became an important item on their diet.

Without the Indians' supplying food, the trade could not have existed. Yet there were times when the larder ran low, and the men were faced with starvation. By boiling their moccasins and pelts, they managed to survive.

Alcoholic beverages, too, became a virtual necessity. The lot of the laborers was hard, and a drink on a regular basis helped make life bearable. The opening of a keg and a dram was a welcome event. Such occasions are reported throughout the fur-trade literature.

Excerpts from the journals of traders throw additional light on their lifestyle. Alexander McKenzie, bourgeois of the XY and NW Companies (not Sir Alexander MacKenzie), gives an account of how things were at Grand Portage before the removal to the Kaministiquia: "The proprietors, clerks, guides, and interpreters, mess together, to the number of sometimes an hundred, at several tables, in one large hall, the provisions consisting of bread, salt pork, beef, hams, fish, and venison, butter, peas, Indian corn, potatoes, tea, spirits, wine, &c, and plenty of milk. Mechanics had the same ration; but canoemen were given no subsistence, here or on the voyage, but corn and grease. The corn was prepared before leaving Detroit by boiling it in lye to take off the husk, when it was washed and dried. It was cooked by boiling it into a sagamity, or hominy, and eaten with salt. A quart of such corn was a ration for 24 hours . . . "

[*Manuscript Journals of Alexander Henry and David Thompson, 1799–1814*, Vol. I, page 248.]

"The nickname '*Le mangeur de bled*' (wheat eater) is an alteration of the term *mangeur de lard*, which was applied with some derision by the Northmen to the voyageurs who paddled between Montreal and Grand Portage without pushing farther into the wilderness. The English translation of the term is 'pork-eater.' The Montreal voyageurs did not live on a diet of hulled corn and tallow, as did the Northmen, but included pork in their rations, a luxury seldom enjoyed in the north country. Huneau [a Frenchman] was apparently still more extravagant, requiring even breadstuffs in his diet." [*Five Fur Traders of the Northwest*, page 68.]

"Corn, beans, pumpkins and other crops are also grown beyond the borders of the Northwest for use in that country. The most important suppliers of these products are the Mandans of the Missouri, and the Ojibwa beyond the Michilimackinac, who also supply maple sugar." [Eric Ross, *Beyond the River and the Bay*, page 76.]

"In the morning we breakfasted most heartily on white fish and buffalo tongues, accompanied by tea, milk, sugar, and galettes, which the voyageurs consider a great luxury. These are cakes made of simple flour and water, and baked by clearing away a place near the fire; the cake is then laid on the hot ground, and covered with ashes, where it is allowed to remain until sufficiently baked. They are very light and pleasant, and are much esteemed." [Paul Kane, *Wanderings of an Artist*, page 258.]

"This grain [wild rice] is gathered in such quantities, in this region, that in ordinary seasons, the North West Company purchase, annually, from twelve to fifteen hundred bushels of it from the Natives; and it constitutes a principal article of food, at the posts in this vicinity." [Daniel Williams Harmon, *Voyages and Travels in the Interior of North America*, page 111.]

"Traded for 10 kegs of sugar and some skins and furs." [*Manuscript Journals of Alexander Henry and David Thompson, 1799–1814*, Vol. I, page 214.]

"The flesh of it [beaver] is very good, either boiled or roasted, but the tail is the best part. While I am upon the subject of dainties, I may add, that the snout of the moose is also highly esteemed." [J. Long, *Voyages and Travels of an Indian Interpreter and Trader*, pages 41–42.]

January 19th, 1806: "While at this post [North West Company] I ate roasted beavers, dressed in every respect as a pig is usually dressed with us; it was excellent. I could not discern the least taste of Des Bois [the wood on which beavers feed.] I also ate boiled moose's head: when well boiled, I consider it equal to the tail of the beaver; in taste and substance they are much alike." [*The Expeditions of Zebulon Montgomery Pike*, Vol. I, page 141.]

"Cartier explored the islands [1535–1536] with his boats, incidentally encountering a friendly group of five savages. One of them, when the boat grounded, picked up the Captain in his arms and carried him ashore 'as if he had been a six-year old child.' These natives were hunting muskrat, of which they had accumulated a great number, and gave Cartier all he and his men wanted to eat; the French found them good." [Samuel Eliot Morison, *The European Discovery of America*, page 411.]

" . . . as the trade extended further and further into the Northwest, the traders became increasingly dependent upon the plains tribes for provisions to supply the ever-lengthening canoe routes." [Eric Ross, *Beyond the River and the Bay*, page 44.]

On the making of pemmican: "The thin slices of dried meat are pounded between two stones until the fibres separate; about 50 lbs. of this are put into a bag of buffalo skin, with about 40 lbs. of melted fat, and mixed together while hot, and sewed up, forming a hard and compact mass; hence its name in the Cree language, *pemmi* signifying meat, and *kon*, fat. Each cart brings home ten of these bags, and all that the half-breeds do not require for themselves is eagerly bought by the Company, for the purpose of sending to the more distant posts, where food is scarce. One pound of this is considered equal to four pounds of ordinary meat, and the pemmican keeps for years perfectly good exposed to any weather." [Paul Kane, *Wanderings of an Artist*, pages 52–53.]

"According to [David] Thompson, pemmican is wholesome, tasty and nutritious, and affords the greatest nourishment for the least possible bulk and weight. Even the gluttonous French Canadians, who devour eight pounds of fresh meat every day, he says, are content with a pound and a half of pemmican per day." [Eric Ross, *Beyond the River and the Bay*, page 77.]

From the diary of Robert Kennicott: "Mr. Hubbard found the nest of a ruffed grouse, containing five eggs. These our cook used in making our *galette*, thereby giving us quite a treat. This galette is the only form of bread used on a voyage, that is, when voyageurs are so fortunate as to have any flour at all. It is made in a very simple style:—the flour bag is opened, and a small hollow made in the flour, into which a little water is poured, and the dough is thus mixed in the bag; nothing is added, except perhaps some dirt from the cook's *unwashed* hands, with which he kneads it into flat cakes, which are baked before the fire in a frying pan, or cooked in grease." [Chicago Academy of Sciences, *Transactions*, Vol. I, part 2, page 154.]

"This lake abounds in sturgeon, which are caught in nets, at all seasons, and on which our people mainly subsist, winter and summer. Wild fowl are also in great abundance, at their proper season." [*Manuscript Journals of Alexander Henry and David Thompson, 1799–1814*, Vol. II, page 476.]

Humphrey Marten, master at York Fort, wrote: "Your Inland Servants in particular think it very hard when they arrive at the Fort to be denied eating as much Provisions (of European kinds and of what sort they like best) as they can. Now there is nothing unhealthy about sleeping in a tent, nor are venison, goose, ptarmigan and fish unwholesome meats." [*Cumberland and Hudson House Journals*, Second Series, page xix.]

"Dandelion greens are especially valued at Churchill where they make an early salad long before anything can be produced in the garden." [Eric Ross, *Beyond the River and the Bay*, page 80.]

"This afternoon our men regaled themselves on the offals of the horses. Puddings were made of the blood and fat. The guts were boiled or roasted, and the marrow-bones cracked—in short, nothing was lost, and had I not seen the horsehides I could have imagined we were just in from a buffalo hunt." [*Manuscript Journals of Alexander Henry and David Thompson, 1799–1814*, Vol. II, page 806.]

A Christmas dinner at Fort Edmonton (1847): "At the head, before Mr. Harriett, was a large dish of buffalo hump; at the foot smoked a boiled buffalo calf. Start not, gentle reader, the calf is very small, and is taken from the cow by the Caesarean operation long before it attains its full growth. This, boiled whole, is one of the most esteemed dishes amongst the epicures of the interior. My pleasing duty was to help a dish of mouffle, or dried moose nose; the gentleman on my left distributed, with graceful impartiality, the white fish, delicately browned in buffalo marrow. The worthy priest helped the buffalo tongue, whilst Mr. Rundell cut up the beavers' tails. Nor was the other gentleman left unemployed, as all his spare time was occupied in dissecting a roast wild goose.

The centre of the table was graced with piles of potatoes, turnips, and bread conveniently placed, so that each could help himself without interrupting the labours of his companions. Such was our jolly Christmas dinner at Edmonton; and long will it remain in my memory, although no pies, or puddings, or blanc manges, shed their fragrance over the scene." [Paul Kane, *Wanderings of an Artist*, page 263.]

"No news from Assiniboine river, except that they are starving at Portage la Prairie, and exist only on esqebois, a root about the thickness and length of a man's finger, which may be termed the wild potato or pomme de terre of this country . . . " [*Manuscript Journals of Alexander Henry and David Thompson, 1799–1814*, Vol. I, page 183.]

DRINK

"In the late 18th and early 19th centuries, before the whole canoe trade fell under the control of the Hudson's Bay Company, it was the custom to distribute 8 gallons of rum to each canoe for consumption during the run, and it was also the custom for all hands to see how much of this they could drink before starting out. This grandiose undertaking usually began as soon as the local priest, who gave his blessing to the canoemen, had left the scene. The magnificient drunk lasted one day and the next morning the crew had to be underway. The first day's run, old accounts repeatedly show, not only was short but was often beset by difficulties." [Edwin T. Adney and Howard I. Chapelle, *The Bark Canoes and Skin Boats of North America*, page 153.]

December 1, 1808: "Denard and Fautienne [Dunord and Fontaine] set off with three kegs of high wine for Fort Augustus. 4th. My hunters and other men have been drinking and rioting since yesterday; they make more d–m noise and trouble than a hundred Blackfeet." [*Manuscript Journals of Alexander Henry and David Thompson, 1799–1814*, Vol. II, page 574.]

"By 2 o'clock P.M. we had reached the Prairie de Thé, a distance of twenty-eight miles. Here we landed to let the men have their customary debauch. In the Hudson's Bay Company's service no rations of liquor are given to the men, either while they are stopping in fort or while travelling, nor are they allowed to purchase any; but when they are about commencing a long journey, the men are given what is called a regale, which consists of a pint of rum each." [Paul Kane, *Wanderings of an Artist*, page 179.]

Fur Trade Site-Seeing

Both Canadians and Americans have witnessed an increased interest in the history of the North American fur trade. To address this new interest, as well as to interpret and preserve the history of the fur trade, the Historic Sites Branch of Parks Canada, the United States National Parks Service, and provincial and state agencies have made a concerted effort to locate, preserve, study, mark and, in many cases, restore or reconstruct historic fur-trade sites.

History and historic sites can be fully understood only when geography or the place becomes a part of the study experience. Therefore, a listing of fur-trade sites in both countries is included. The list is based upon information supplied by the Historic Sites Branch of Parks Canada, the U. S. National Park Service, Canadian provinces, and a number of states. The history of fur-trade sites and their locations can be difficult and complex. Some posts existed for only a season and others for longer periods of time. Some moved to nearby locations, while others were taken over by competitors. When the North West Company merged with the Hudson's Bay Company, all North West Company posts fell under the aegis of the Hudson's Bay Company.

The following key will indicate the administrative or historic status of the site:

Parks Canada (federal) – PC
U.S. National Park Service (federal) – NPS
Canadian provincial – P
State (U.S.) – S
North West Company – NWC
XY Company – XYC
Hudson's Bay Company – HBC
Historic Sites and Monuments Board of Canada – HSMB
Minnesota Historical Society – MHS

CANADA (by province east to west)

Nova Scotia

Champlain's Habitation, Port Royal (reconstructed) – PC
Fort St. Peters, St. Peters (plaque)

New Brunswick

Fort Jemseg, Lower Jemseg (plaque) – HSMB
Fort La Tour, St. John

Quebec

Fort Temiscamingue, Villa Marie (ruins and cemetery) – PC
Cartier-Brebeuf, National Historic Park, Quebec City (replica of Cartier's Flagship) – PC
Chaudière Portages on the Ottawa River, Hull (plaque) – HSMB
Fort Trois-Rivières, Trois Rivières (plaque) – HSMB
Tadoussac, Tadoussac, French and North West Company (plaque) – HSMB
Rupert House, Rupert House, originally Charles Fort (plaque) – HBC
Musée Chauvin, Tadoussac (reconstruction of early trading post)
fief Pachiriny, Place d' Armes, Trois Rivières (location of the great annual fur fair, plaque)
Château Ramezay, Montreal (built by Compagnies des Indes Occidantales about 1756) French regime
Simon Fraser home (NWC), 153 rue Sainte-Anne, Sainte-Anne-de-Bellevue, P.O. Quebec

Ontario

Fort St. Joseph, St. Joseph's Island, NWC (ruins) – PC
Old Fort William, Thunder Bay, NWC (complete reconstruction) – P
Fort William, Thunder Bay, original site, NWC (plaque)
French River, Highway 69 and bridge, historic waterway of the fur trade (plaque)
Bay of Quinte Carrying Place, Carrying Place (plaque) – HSMB
Ermatinger House, Sault Ste. Marie (visible structure) – HSMB
Fort Frontenac, Kingston (plaque) – HSMB
Fort St. Pierre, Fort Frances, French (plaque) – HSMB
Inverarden House, Cornwall (plaque) – HSMB
Kaministiquia Route, Thunder Bay, 1688 (plaque) – HSMB
Mattawa Route, Mattawa (plaque) – HSMB
Moose Factory, Moose Factory (visible structures, plaque) – HBC – HSMB
Fort Albany, Fort Albany, accessible by water and air only (original site) – HBC
Niagara Portage Road, Stamford (plaque) – HSMB

Canoe Lock, Sault Ste. Marie, NWC (visible structure)

Fort Frances, Fort Frances, HBC (plaque)

Lac La Pluie Post, Fort Frances, NWC (plaque)

Rat Portage Post, Kenora, Old Fort Island, NWC and HBC (plaque at the bridge on Highway 17)

Manitoba

Lower Fort Garry, Selkirk, HBC (restored stone fort)—PC

Fort Prince of Wales, Churchill, HBC (substantial ruins)—PC

Norway House, Norway House, HBC, accessible by water and float plane (buildings)—PC

Seven Oakes House, Winnipeg (restored, plaque)

Oxford House, Oxford Lake—HBC

York Factory, York Factory, HBC, depot building, accessible by canoe and float plane (plaque)—PC

Upper Fort Garry, Winnipeg, HBC (ruins of one stone gate), City of Winnipeg

Forts Rouge, Garry and Gibralter, Winnipeg, NWC and HBC (plaques)

Fort Churchill, Churchill, HBC (plaque)—HSMB

Fort Dauphin, Winnipegosis, French (plaque)—HSMB

Fort Douglas, Winnipeg, HBC (plaque)—HSMB

Fort La Reine, Portage la Prairie, French (plaque)—HSMB

Fore Maurepas, Pine Falls, French (plaque)—HSMB

Souris-Assiniboine Posts, Wawahesa, HBC, NWC and XYC (plaques)—HSMB

Fort des Epinettes, Pine Fort (plaque)—P

Saskatchewan

Sturgeon Fort, Prince Albert, NWC (cairn and cellars)—PC

Fort Esperance, Spy Hill, near Rocanville, NWC (monument and cellars)—PC

Fort Pelly, Pelly, HBC (ruins)—PC

Cumberland Lake and House, Cumberland Lake, free-trader, HBC, NWC (visible structures)

Fort Carlton, Carlton, HBC (partial reconstruction and plaque)—HSMB

Fort Pitt, Fort Pitt Provincial Park, HBC (plaque)—HSMB

Fort Qu'Appelle, Fort Qu'Appelle, HBC (plaque)—HSMB

Frog Portage, Churchill River (plaque)—HSMB

Ile-à-la Crosse, Ile à-la-Crosse, free-trader, NWC and HBC (plaque)—HSMB

Methye Portage, 13 miles, Lac La Loche, free-trader, XYC, NWC, HBC (plaque)—HSMB

Alberta

Rocky Mountain House posts, Rocky Mountain House, NWC and HBC (ruins)—PC

Fort Chipewyan I, Old Fort Point on Lake Athabasca, NWC, on Indian land, accessible by float plane or boat

Fort Chipewyan II, Fort Chipewyan, Lake Athabasca cairn and cellar pits, NWC and HBC—PC

Fort Edmonton, Edmonton, HBC (reconstructed), owned by City of Edmonton

Fort Augustus, NWC, and Edmonton House, HBC, near Fort Saskatchewan Settlement (plaque)—HSMB

Fort Dunvegan, Dunvegan (visible structure and plaque)—HSMB

Fort Fork, junction of the Smokey and Peace rivers, NWC and HBC (cairn and plaque)—HSMB

Jasper House, Jasper National Park, HBC (plaque)—HSMB

Fort George—Buckingham House, 10 miles southeast of Elk Point, NWC and HBC (cairns)

Fort Vermilion, highway 897 and the North Saskatchewan River, NWC and HBC (cairn and cellars)

Lac La Biche Post, Lac La Biche, NWC and HBC (cairn)

British Columbia

Fort Langley, Langley (reconstructed)—PC

Fort St. James, Fort St. James, NWC and HBC (buildings)—PC

Fort Alexandria, 25 miles south of Quesnel, HBC (plaque)—HSMB

Fort Hope, Hope, HBC (plaque)—HSMB

Fort Kamloops, Kamloops, HBC (plaque)—HSMB

Fort McLeod, Fort McLeod, NWC (ruins and plaque)—HSMB

Forts St. John, near Taylor, NWC (plaque)—HSMB

Fort Victoria, Victoria, HBC (plaque)—HSMB

Kootenae House, Invermere, NWC (plaque)—HSMB

Fort Rupert, Fort Rupert, HBC (visible structure)—HSMB

Fort George, Prince George, NWC (reconstructed, palisade and marker)

Fort Fraser, Fort Fraser, NWC and HBC (marker)

Boat Encampment, 90 miles north of Revelstoke, NWC (marker)

S. S. Beaver, Vancouver, fur trade vessel (marker and exhibit)

Northwest Territories

Fort McPherson, Fort McPherson, HBC (plaque)—HSMB

Fort Reliance, Reliance, HBC (structure)

Fort Resolution, Fort Resolution, HBC

Fort Simpson, Fort Simpson, NWC and HBC (plaque)—HSMB

Fort Aklavik, Mackenzie River delta, HBC

UNITED STATES (alphabetical)

Colorado

Bent's Fort, 35110 Highway 194 E, La Junta—NPS

Fort Vasques, US 85, one mile south of Platteville—S

Illinois

Fort de Chartres, 4 miles west of Prairie du Rocher on the Mississippi River (one original structure and several reconstructed)

Pierre Menard Home, Ellis Grove (finest example of French colonial architecture)

Indiana

Fort Ouiatenon, Lafayette

Michel Brouillet Home, Vincennes

Michigan

Fort Michilimackinac, Mackinaw City, French, free traders and NWC (reconstruction)—Mackinac Island State Park Commission

Fort Mackinac, Mackinac Island (visible structures)—Mackinac Island State Park Commission

Robert Stuart House, Mackinac Island (visible structure)—Mackinac Island State Park Commission

John Johnston and Henry Schoolcraft houses, Sault Ste. Marie (structures)

Fort Pontchartrain, Detroit

Minnesota

Grand Portage, 8½ mile portage, Grand Portage, French, free traders and NWC (partial reconstruction)–NPS

Fort St. Charles, Northwest Angle, French

John Sayer Post, NWC, Pine City (reconstruction)–MHS

Fort Snelling, St. Paul-Minneapolis (reconstruction and several original structures)–MHS

Savanna Portage, near Big Sandy Lake, Highway 65, north of Aitkin–S

Faribault House, Mendota, American Fur Co. (original structure)

Fort Charlotte, west end of Grand Portage, NWC and XYC –NPS

Missouri

Felix Valle Home, Ste. Genevieve (original structure)

Fort Charrette building, Washington (restored)

Nebraska

Fort Atkinson, 10 miles north of Omaha

Museum of the Fur Trade, Chadron

New York

Albany (terminus of the Dutch fur trade in the 17th century)

North Dakota

Fort Union, confluence of the Missouri and Yellowstone rivers –NPS

Oregon

John McLoughlin house, Oregon City

Fort Astoria, Astoria (plaque)

Fort Clatsop, Astoria

South Dakota

Fort Pierre Chouteau trading post, 3 miles north of Fort Pierre (plaque)

Utah

Deserter Point Mountain Green Trapper Confrontation Site, Weber Canyon along Interstate 80, Mountain Green

Washington

Fort Vancouver, Vancouver (visible structure)–NPS

Fort Nisqually, Tacoma

Wisconsin

Villa Louis, Prairie du Chien, American Fur Co. (visible structure)–S

Yellow River, between Webster and Danbury (reconstructed), NWC and XYC sites

Astor Warehouse, Prairie du Chien, American Fur Co. (visible structure)–S

Brisbois House, Prairie du Chien, American Fur Co. (visible structure)–S

Brule-St. Croix Portage, 2 miles northeast of Solon Springs

Fox-Wisconsin Portage, Portage (plaque)

Wyoming

Fort Laramie, Fort Laramie

South Pass, state Highway 28 between Farson and Lander (plaque)

Green River Rendezvous, US 191 and State 354 west of Pinedale

Fort Bridger, 32 miles west of Evanston

Conclusion

It is the author's hope that the purposes mentioned in the foreword have been achieved; that the reader has acquired a greater appreciation of fur-trade artifacts as sources of history. By necessity, there are omissions, as the materials sold and used in the fur trade were many. It is hoped that the use of manuscripts and books, together with objects illustrated here, has demonstrated the importance of utilizing as many sources as possible as we try to understand the past.

Two historical archaeologists–a Canadian and an American–have suggested adding a statement about the damage that can result from the unlawful removal of objects from, or the excavation of, prehistoric or historic sites by non-professionals. In the last few years especially, great damage has occurred through the use of metal detectors and the non-reporting of underground, underwater or surface finds. An object or artifact by itself, removed from the exact location where it was found, is of little importance or value to the archaeologist. By such removal, an important part of its story is lost to history. Knowing where it was found, and in what association with other materials, is vital.

Suggested Reading

Bolz, J. Arnold. *Portage into the Past*. Minneapolis: University of Minnesota Press, 1960.

Brebner, John Bartlet. *The Explorers of North America, 1492–1806*. Garden City, N.Y.: Doubleday, 1955.

Campbell, Marjorie Wilkins. *The North West Company*. Toronto: Macmillan Company of Canada, 1957.

Coues, Eliott, ed. *The Manuscript Journals of Alexander Henry and David Thompson, 1799–1814*. 2 vols. Minneapolis: Ross & Haines, 1965.

Eccles, W. J. *The Canadian Frontier, 1534–1760*. Toronto: Holt, Rinehart and Winston, 1969.

Gates, Charles M., ed. *Five Fur Traders of the Northwest*. St. Paul: Minnesota Historical Society, 1965.

Gilman, Carolyn. *Where Two Worlds Meet*. St. Paul: Minnesota Historical Society, 1982.

Hanson, Charles E., Jr. *The Northwest Gun*. Lincoln, Nebraska State Historical Society, 1957.

Hanson, James A. *Voyageur's Sketchbook*. Chadron, Nebraska: The Fur Press, 1981.

Henry, Alexander. *Travels and Adventures in Canada and the Indian Territories Between the Years 1760 and 1776*. Edmonton: M. G. Hurtig, 1969.

Innis, Harold A. *The Fur Trade in Canada*. Toronto: University of Toronto Press, 1956.

Lavender, David. *The Fist in the Wilderness*. New York: Doubleday, 1964.

Morse, Eric. *Fur Trade Canoe Routes of Canada/Then and Now*. Ottawa: Queen's Printer and Controller of Stationery, 1969.

Nute, Grace Lee. *The Voyageur*. St. Paul: Minnesota Historical Society, 1955.

Ray, Arthur J. *Indians in the Fur Trade: their role as hunters, trappers and middlemen in the lands southwest of Hudson Bay, 1660–1870*. Toronto: University of Toronto Press, 1974.

Rich, E. E., ed. *Hudson's Bay Company, 1670–1870*. 2 vols. London: Hudson's Bay Record Society, 1958–1959.

Van Kirk, Sylvia. *"Many Tender Ties": Women in the Fur-Trade Society in Western Canada, 1670–1870*. Winnipeg: Watson & Dwyer, 1980.

Wallace, W. Stewart. *The Pedlars from Quebec*. Toronto: Ryerson Press, 1954.

Wheeler, Robert C., et al. *Voices from the Rapids: An Underwater Search for Fur-Trade Artifacts, 1960–1973*. St. Paul: Minnesota Historical Society, 1975.

Bibliography

Books

Adney, Edwin Tappen, and Howard I. Chapelle. *The Bark Canoes and Skin Boats of North America*. Washington, D.C.: Smithsonian Institution, 1964.

Bardon, Richard, and Grace Lee Nute, eds. *A Winter in the St. Croix Valley: George Nelson's Reminiscences, 1802–03*. St. Paul: Minnesota Historical Society, 1948.

Biggar, H. P. *The Early Trading Companies of New France*. New York: Argonaut Press, 1965.

Bouchard, Russel. *Les fusils de Tulle en Nouvelle-France: 1691–1741*. Chicoutimi, Quebec: Journal des Armes enr., 1980.

Boulanger, Tom. *An Indian Remembers: My Life as a Trapper in Northern Manitoba*. Winnipeg: Peguis Publishers, 1971.

Brain, Jeffrey P. *Tunica Treasure*. Cambridge and Salem: The Peabody Museum of Archaeology and Ethnology, Harvard University and the Peabody Museum of Salem, 1979.

Brebner, John Bartlet. *The Explorers of North America, 1492–1806*. Garden City, N.Y.: Doubleday, 1955.

Brown, M. L. *Firearms in Colonial America, 1492–1792*. Washington City: Smithsonian Press, 1980.

Burpee, Lawrence J., ed. *Journals and Letters of Pierre Gaultier de Varennes, Sieur de La Vérendrye and His Sons*. Toronto: Champlain Society. Vol. XVI, 1927.

Chalmers, J. W. *Fur Trade Governor: George Simpson, 1820–1860*. Edmonton, Alberta: The Institute of Applied Art, 1960.

Couses, Elliott, ed. *The Manuscript Journals of Alexander Henry and David Thompson, 1799–1814*. 2 volumes. Minneapolis: Ross & Haines, 1965.

——, ed. *Zebulon M. Pike Expeditions in the Years 1805-6-7*. Minneapolis: Ross & Haines, 1965.

Davies, K. G., ed. *Letters from Hudson Bay, 1703–1740*. London: Hudson's Bay Record Society, 1965.

Densmore, Frances. "Uses of Plants by the Chippewa Indians." *Forty-Fourth Annual Report of the Bureau of Ethnology to the Secretary of the Smithsonian Institution, 1926–1927*. Washington: Government Printing Office, 1928.

Denys, Nicolas. *The Description and Natural History of the Coasts of North America (Acadia)*, trans. and ed. by William F. Ganong. Toronto: Champlain Society, 1908.

Eccles, W. J. *The Canadian Frontier, 1534–1760*. Toronto: Holt, Rinehart and Winston, 1969.

Franklin, John. *Journey to the Shores of the Polar Sea in 1819–20–21–22: with a Brief Account of the Second Journey in 1825–26–27*. 4 vols. London: John Murray, 1829.

Fredrickson, N. Jaye, and Sandra Gibb. *The Covenant Chain: Indian Ceremonial and Trade Silver*. Ottawa: National Museum of Canada, 1980.

Garry, Nicholas. "Diary of Nicholas Garry." *Proceedings and Transactions of the Royal Society of Canada*. 2nd Series, Vol. VI. Montreal: Gazette Printing Company, 1900.

Gates, Charles M., ed. *Five Fur Traders of the Northwest*. St. Paul: Minnesota Historical Society, 1965.

Gentilhomme, Guy. *Revillon, 1723–1973*. Paris: Revillon Frères, 1973.

Gérin-Lajoie, Marie, and Kenneth Kidd. "Montreal Merchants' Records, 1708–1775." MSS: Minnesota Historical Society, St. Paul.

Gilman, Carolyn. *Where Two Worlds Meet: the great lakes fur trade*. St. Paul: Minnesota Historical Society, 1982.

Good, Mary Elizabeth. *Guebert Site: an 18th Century Historic Kaskaskia Indian Village*. Wood River, Illinois: Central States Archaeological Societies, 1972.

Guillet, Edwin C. *Pioneer Travel in Upper Canada*. Toronto: University of Toronto Press, 1963.

Hamilton, T. M. *Colonial Frontier Guns*. Chadron, Nebraska: Fur Press, 1980.

Hankins, Col. *Dakota Land; or, The Beauty of St. Paul*. New York: Hankins and Son, 1868.

Hanson, Charles E., Jr. *The Northwest Gun*. Lincoln: Nebraska State Historical Society, 1955.

Hargrave, Catherine Perry. *A History of Playing Cards and a Bibliography of Cards and Gaming*. New York: Dover Publicatons, 1966.

Harmon, Daniel Williams. *A Journal of Voyages and Travels in the Interior of North America*. Toronto: Courier Press, 1911.

Henry, Alexander. *Travels and Adventures in Canada and the Indian Territories Between the Years 1760 and 1776*. Edmonton: M. G. Hurtig, 1969.

Heriot, George. *Travels Through the Canadas*. Vols. 1 and 2. London: Richard Phillips, 1807.

Hume, Ivor Noël. *A Guide to Artifacts of Colonial America*. New York: Alfred A. Knopf, 1970.

Innis, Harold A. *The Fur Trade in Canada*. Toronto: University of Toronto Press, 1956.

Johnson, Eldon. *The Prehistoric Peoples of Minnesota*. St. Paul: Minnesota Historical Society, 1978.

Johnston, Patricia Condon. *Eastman Johnson's Lake Superior Indians*. Afton, Minnesota: Johnston Publishing, 1983.

Kane, Paul. *Wanderings of an Artist among the Indians of North America*. Edmonton: M. G. Hurtig, 1968.

Kennicott, Robert. *Narrative of Robert Kennicott*. Transactions of the Chicago Academy of Sciences. Vol. 1, part 2. Chicago: Academy of Sciences, 1869.

Kenyon, W. A. *The Grimsby Site: A Historic Neutral Cemetery*. Toronto: Royal Ontario Museum, 1982.

Kerr, D. G. G., ed. *A Historical Atlas of Canada*. Toronto: Thomas Nelson & Sons, 1960.

Kidd, Kenneth and Marie Gérin-Lajoie. "Montreal Merchants' Records, 1708–1775." MSS: Minnesota Historical Society, St. Paul.

Lamb, W. Kaye, ed. *The Journals and Letters of Sir Alexander Mackenzie*. Toronto: Macmillan of Canada, 1970.

——, ed. *Simon Fraser Letters and Journals, 1806–1808*. Toronto: Macmillan of Canada, 1960.

Leacock, Eleanor Burke, and Nancy Oestreich Lurie, eds. *North American Indians in Historical Perspective*. New York: Random House, Inc., 1971.

Leechman, Douglas. *Native Tribes of Canada*. Toronto: W. J. Gage, n.d.

Long, J. *Voyages and Travels of an Indian Interpreter and Trader, Describing the Manners and Customs of the North American Indians with an Account of the Posts Situated on the River Saint Laurence, Lake Ontario, &c*. London: 1791; rpt. Toronto: Coles Publishing Company, 1971.

Mactaggart, John. *Three Years in Canada: An Account of the Actual State of the Country in 1826-7-8*. 2 vols. London: Henry Colburn, 1829.

McGillivray, Robert, and George B. *A History of the Clan Macgillivray*. Thunder Bay: George Macgillivray, 1973.

Masson, L. R. *Les Bourgeois de la Compagnie du Nord-Ouest*. 2 vols. New York: Antiquarian Press, 1960.

McLean, John. *John McLean's Notes of a Twenty-Five Year Service in the Hudson's Bay Territory*, ed. W. A. Wallace. Toronto: Champlain Society, 1932.

Miller, J. Jefferson, and Lyle M. Stone. *Eighteenth-Century Ceramics From Fort Michilimackinac: A Study in Historical Archaeology*. Washington, D.C.: Smithsonian Institution Press, 1970.

Morison, Samuel Eliot. *The European Discovery of America: The Northern Voyages, A.D. 500–1600*. New York: Oxford University Press, 1971.

Morse, Eric W. *Fur Trade Canoe Routes of Canada/Then and Now*. Ottawa: Queen's Printer and Controller of Stationery, 1969.

Morton, Arthur S. *A History of the Canadian West to 1870–71*. Toronto: University of Toronto Press, 1973.

Nish, Cameron. *The French Regime*. Scarborough, Ontario: Prentice-Hall of Canada, 1965.

Patterson II, E. Palmer. *The Canadian Indian: A History Since 1500*. Don Mills, Ontario: Collier-Macmillan Canada, 1972.

Perrault, Jean Baptiste. "Narrative of the Travels and Adventures of a Merchant Voyageur in the Savage Territories of Northern America Leaving Montreal the 28th of May 1783." *Historical Collections and Researches made by the Michigan Pioneer and Historical Society*. Vol. 37. Lansing: 1909–1910.

Petersen, Eugene T. *Gentlemen on the Frontier: A Pictorial Record of the Culture of Michilimackinac*. Mackinac Island, Michigan: Mackinac Island State Park Commission, 1964.

Ray, Arthur J. *Indians in the Fur Trade: their role as hunters, trappers and middlemen in the lands southwest of Hudson Bay, 1660–1870*. Toronto: University of Toronto Press, 1974.

Rich, E. E., ed. *Cumberland and Hudson House Journals, 1775–1782*. 2 vols. London: Hudson's Bay Record Society, 1951–1952.

——, ed. *Hudson's Bay Company, 1670–1870*. 2 vols. London: Hudson's Bay Record Society, 1958–1959.

Roberts, Kenneth G., and Philip Shackleton. *The Canoe: A History of the Craft from Panama to the Arctic*. Camden, Maine: International Marine Publishing Company, 1983.

Ross, Eric. *Beyond the River and the Bay: Some Observations on the State of the Canadian Northwest in 1811*. Toronto: University of Toronto Press, 1970.

Russell, Carl P. *Firearms, Traps & Tools of the Mountain Men.* New York: Alfred A. Knopf, 1967.

Saum, Lewis O. *The Fur Trader and the Indian.* Seattle and London: University of Washington Press, 1965.

Seymour, E. S. *Sketches of Minnesota: The New England of the West.* New York: Harper & Brothers, 1850.

Tanner, Ogden. *The Canadians.* Alexandria, Virginia: Time-Life, 1977.

Thompson, David. *David Thompson's Narrative of His Explorations in Western America, 1784–1812,* ed. J. B. Tyrrell. Toronto: Champlain Society, 1916.

Thompson, Erwin N. *Grand Portage: The Great Carrying Place—A History of the Site, People, and Fur Trade.* Washington, D.C. : U.S. Department of Interior, 1969.

Trudel, Marcel. *The Beginnings of New France, 1524–1663.* Toronto: McClelland and Stewart, 1973.

Umfreville, Edward. *The Present State of Hudson's Bay—Containing a Full Description of that Settlement, and the Adjacent Country; and Likewise of the Fur Trade.* Toronto: Ryerson Press, 1954.

Van Kirk, Sylvia. *"Many Tender Ties": Women in Fur-Trade Society in Western Canada, 1670–1870.* Winnipeg: Watson & Dwyer, 1980.

Voorhis, Ernest, comp. *Historic Forts and Trading Posts of the French Regime and of the English Fur-Trading Companies.* Ottawa: Canadian Department of the Interior, 1930.

Walker, Iain. *Clay Tobacco Pipes, With Particular Reference to the Bristol Industry.* Vol. 4. Ottawa: Parks Canada, 1977.

Wallace, W. Stewart. *The Pedlars from Quebec and Other Papers on the Nor'Westers.* Toronto: Ryerson Press, 1954.

——, ed. *Documents Relating to the North West Company.* Toronto: Champlain Society, 1934.

Wheeler, Robert C., Walter Kenyon, Alan Woolworth and Douglas Birk. *Voices from the Rapids: An Underwater Search for Fur-Trade Artifacts, 1960–1973.* St. Paul: Minnesota Historical Society, 1975.

Woodward, Arthur. *Denominators of the Fur Trade: An Anthology of Writings on the Material Culture of the Fur Trade.* Pasadena: Socio-Technical Publications, 1970.

Magazines and Periodicals

Anderson, Thomas G. "Personal Narrative of Capt. Thomas G. Anderson." *Wisconsin Historical Collections,* vol. 9, pp. 137–206.

Birmingham Public Library, Birmingham, England. Letter to the author, December 23, 1971.

Forman, James D. "Guns of the American Indians." *The Canadian Journal of Arms Collecting,* 2:4:107, 1973.

Glover, R. "York Boats." *The Beaver,* March, 1949, pp. 19–23.

Hanson, Charles E., Jr., Letter to the author, December 20, 1971.

Hart, Irving H. "The Old Savanna Portage." *Minnesota History,* June, 1927, pp. 125–126.

Hudson's Bay Company, Winnipeg. Letter to the author, March 30, 1983.

Mackay, Douglas. "Blanket Coverage." *The Beaver,* June, 1935, pp. 45–52.

Nyholm, Earl, assistant professor of Ojibwa, Bemidji State University. Letter to the author, May 18, 1983.

Payne, Michael, and Gregory Thomas. "Literacy, Literature and Libraries in the Fur Trade." *The Beaver,* Spring, 1983, pp. 44–53.

Trillin, Calvin. "U.S. Journal: Louisiana—The Tunica Treasure." *The New Yorker,* July 27, 1981, pp. 41–50.

Wharton, T. Letter to the author, November 18, 1972.

Williams, Glydwr. "Highlights in the History of the First Two Hundred Years of the Hudson's Bay Company." *The Beaver,* Autumn, 1970, pp. 4–59.

Wilson, Clifford P. "The Beaver Club." *The Beaver,* March 1936, pp. 19–24.

The doodles inside the front and back covers are the work of Alexis Bailly, American Fur Company trader, and are found in Volume 41 of his Indian credit book. This and other Bailly papers are in the manuscript department of the Minnesota Historical Society.

Alexis Bailly was born at St. Joseph in 1798 near the Canadian shore of Lake Huron, of French and Ottawa Indian background. He received a good education at Montreal, and for a part of his life was engaged in the fur trade. In August, 1821, Bailly drove cattle from Fort Snelling to the Red River settlement. In 1828 he settled at Prairie du Chien, and in 1833 moved to Mendota. Three years later he moved to Wabasha, Minnesota. Bailly served as a member of the first Minnesota Territorial legislature. He died in Wabasha in 1861.

It is believed that the doodles appearing here were done while Bailly was engaged in the fur trade at St. Peters (now Mendota, Minnesota).

Biographical material is from an unpublished manuscript by Walter Belliveau, "The Life of Alexis Bailly: Minnesota Pioneer," at the Minnesota Historical Society.

Printed by Viking Press, Inc.
Eden Prairie, MN

The Second Printing of this book is to honor my late parents, Robert C. Wheeler and Ardis M. Wheeler, author and editor of this text and yours truly.

Jonathan Wheeler